PALPABLE DISCORD
a year of drama and Chelsea

for Angela and Charl.

Clayton Beerman is relatively new to the writing game, but a couple of years ago he caught the bug. An article here and there, and then some podcasts -- and now a book. He first went to Chelsea in 1968 although he had already seen them live in 1967 at a ground in north London where a team in white play. He was taken by his Uncle who tried and failed to get him to support that team. Clayton's had a season ticket at Stamford Bridge for more years than he cares to remember but cherishes the memories and friendships that have formed from his love of the Blues.

Follow Clayton Beerman on Twitter @goalie59

Palpable Discord

a year of drama and dissent at Chelsea

CLAYTON BEERMAN

Palpable Discord

PUBLISHED BY GATE 17
www.gate17.co.uk

enquiries@gate17.co.uk
cover photograph Clayton Beerman
cover design GATE 17

CONTENTS

AUTHOR'S NOTE

There was a moment during the last game of the season where one of my mates said to another, "don't ask him, he knows nothing!" Not perhaps the most flattering observation about my views, and it was true drink had been taken, but we were at the time having the "stay or go" conversation while watching the boys in blue draw at home to the Champions.

That as we know is the beauty of football. Everyone has an opinion, and all of them are valid to some degree because they are what you believe. This book is made up of my opinions on Chelsea Football Club's 2015/2016 Premier League season and includes my articles from the Chelsea Football Fancast website, and some from the cfcuk fanzine both of which I am honoured to write for. Those articles have been updated and I have added extra material which includes a season and player review, a final look at Jose, and a look back at where it all started. I hope that you enjoy the book (as opposed to the actual season) and let me know what you think.

I would like to thank Mark Worrall of Gate 17 for his enthusiasm and support of this project and love of hot chocolate, to David Chidgey for hosting my articles on the Chelsea Fancast website and for allowing me to spout my pearls of wisdom on the fancast, to David Johnstone, to Tim Rolls, to Jonny, Tony, Mark and Donal for letting me sit in their Podding Shed. To the guys I spend so much of my time watching Chelsea with -- Andy S, Andy A, Istvan and Mark. To Howard Parnes RIP.

These things however can never be done without the love and support of loved ones so thank you to them for the encouragement and indulgence in letting me indulge this love you know who you are.

CORNWALL

July 2015

An email came through on the 29th July 2015, it was from the London Standard. My friend Jonny Dyer had given my name to a journalist who asked if I'd do a season preview. How could I say no, my first exposure to the press if you don't include a picture of me in a crowd scene in rag week at Harrow Tech.

I was on holiday in Cornwall at the time, but with an iPad propped up on one knee and dodgy WIFI reception I went about my predictions. Now before you laugh, just think what yours would have been at that very same time.

Here are the questions.

- What's your target for the club's forthcoming season?
- Which one player would you like to see your club sign before the transfer window closes?
- Which fixture are you most looking forward to?
- Which signing are you most excited about?
- Which young player excites you the most?
- Who's the most important player in your team?
- Who's the weak link in your team?

- Which opposing player will get booed the most at your ground?

So cast your mind back and try and think what you would have said?

- I said my hopes were retaining the title but I'd really like to win the FA Cup again. I predicted we'd be champions…..
- I said I'd like to sign Marco Veratti, but I didn't think anyone else would come in.
- The fixture I was most looking forward to was Spurs, oh boy was that to come true.
- I said that in the absence of any major signings, the best signing we had made was Jose to a new 4 year deal.
- I predicted the breakthrough star would be Bertrand Traore
- I said our most important player is Eden Hazard.
- As for our weaknesses, I feared for our defence and particularly the ball behind our full backs.
- The player that would get booed, I plumped for Rafa if he ever came back with Real Madrid (I got that horribly wrong or more accurately he did)

So not a bad effort, but little did I know. In my worst nightmare I couldn't have believed the season that has just ended. A season without silverware is not and will never be a disaster. I am of an age where I will never have or "enjoy" a sense of entitlement, but if a certain beer company did football seasons, it wouldn't be this one.

We have yet again let the best manager in the club's history go and ended up with a bunch of players who quite frankly don't give a toss. There are a few exceptions but as a club we have been immune in the main from the mercenaries but not this year. The short term nature of the management of the club has finally come home to roost.

There has been the bizarre lack of any concerted effort to integrate the best group of youth players in a generation into the first team, and an unfathomable transfer policy.

It has been an interesting exercise looking back. My positive support for certain players looks a little naïve, but there was nothing wrong with giving them the benefit of the doubt was there? It seems my favourite underachievers were Oscar and Thibaut, banging the drum for youth and my unwavering support for Jose. Having just watched him hold up his Manchester United shirt I feel nothing but regret and upset.

One thing that has really hit home is the power of social media. The blame culture "it's this one's fault" "Emenalo Out", "the Rats", "sign JT", "why did we do this?", "we should be doing that". All things picked up by the press and the insatiable thirst for stories. Someone said we get the press that we deserve and that still rings true. Some of the agenda driven nonsense put out by some journalists is divisive and meant to reel in those gullible to respond.

There are so many outlets and so many conduits for people's voices. I use several, the websites, the fanzine and the podcasts. They are in essence the 21st century pub conversations or the playground rows. At the end of the day it's driven by love for the game and for the club. It's a different world to when I started watching football, but at the end of the day I still get the tingle when I walk through the vastly different "gates" of Stamford Bridge. I still get excited by that blue shirt, and despite all the doom and gloom cannot wait for the arrival of Mr Conte

So this is my journey and thoughts on the 2015/2016 but let's start at the very beginning....

WOULD YOUR DAUGHTER LIKE A DRINK?

1967

The game at home following Jose's sacking was significant for many things, it also fell on the second anniversary of my Dad's passing. It got me thinking about my own passage of becoming a Chelsea fan and the part taken by my Dad.

Dad's brother supported Spurs and so my first few live games were watched at that place in North London where the team in white play. My first ever Chelsea game was 1967. Famous both for my first appearance and the goal scoring debut of Chico Hamilton. My first home games were in 1968, a draw at home to Newcastle and a win against already relegated QPR. I went with a family friend Howard. He lived in Brighton and I was taken by him to those games whilst on holiday there. We sat in the East Stand and I remember the mass of people and my first real journey on the tube. The most vivid memory was being hauled up by my arm between platform and track when getting on the train at Fulham Broadway!

I can't remember the first game my Dad took me to but I suspect it may have been the FA Cup semi-final at that place mentioned above. We won 5-1 and

I had managed to bite my nails through my gloves. I remember turning to him and asking in wonderment whether that meant we were going to be playing at Wembley.

I then remember, probably after huge badgering, that a half season, season ticket was purchased in 1971. It was in the front row of the old East Stand right in the corner at the shed end. Not many games stand out except I do remember us losing at home to Burnley on a Monday night. It must have been school holiday time, but a 0-1 defeat on a night we were expected to win was proper Chelsea.

We went to a few home games together with my younger brother Jamie. A particular treat as we lunched in Dinos, an Italian restaurant next to Fulham Broadway Station. Our respective blue and white scarves carried spaghetti sauces stains for years afterwards like a badge of honour. Through Howard's connections with Dave Sexton, his wife would often join us for lunch together with Peter Bonetti's wife. One particular thrill was seeing the bones of a dead bird (possibly a dove) which Dave Sexton had throughout the 70s cup run as his lucky charm.

In that 1971 season as cup holders, I remember the crushing disappointment of losing to Everton in the curtain raiser Charity Shield played at the Bridge. The sight of the FA cup being paraded pre game scant consolation! Later that season, as cup holders, we went crashing out to Manchester City in the 4th round at home to a very good Manchester City side and not only was my Dad there, so was my grandfather… a card carrying Millwall fan. His laughter as we left the ground early 0-3 down was not one of my happiest childhood memories.

One thing that my Dad did which drove me and my brother mad was he would always leave early. He hated being stuck in traffic and in those days quite a few people drove as there were no parking restrictions to speak of which is hard to imagine these days. So we would get hauled out with at least 10 minutes to go. I remember craning my neck to get every last second. The number of times that we heard the roar of a goal on our way back to the car! It probably wasn't that many, but it certainly felt like it. I do know for a fact that we left one game at 0-0, and by the time we got back to the car we'd won 2-1. I suspect had my Dad been at the home game with Everton this year we may have been home before JT equalised in the 97th minute.

The only thing in his defence was we invariably got home in time for Dr Who. This was of course before the days of any form of recording devices, and so if you missed it that was that!

The biggest game of that season for me was the semi-final of the Cup Winners Cup at home to Manchester City again. A midweek win against

Manchester City with Derek Smethurst getting the winner. Not only was my Dad there but also my Mum. That being the case we must have left very early that night. That wasn't Mum's last appearance. The whole family attended Peter Bonetti's testimonial game against Standard Liege. My brother and I had these pendants with the "Cats" face on it which we wore round our necks. We had "VIP" seats as Howard was on the testimonial committee. A warm summer's night a great time had by all and of course in true Chelsea style, a defeat. I do however still retain the programme and the signed poster acquired by Dad at the testimonial dinner.

One game I didn't get to was the Bruge game in the Cup Winners Cup run. It was the second leg and we were 2-0 down. It was a big ask but it was the return of Peter Osgood who had been banned for 8 games. He had a huge Afro on the go and massive sideburns. I only know those things now through photos, no TV coverage then.

I was desperate to go but had been ill with a bad bout of flu and that together with it being a school night had me confined to bed. My Dad went and as I understand it now the game was one of those, wish I'd been there nights. We drew back to 2-0 in normal time and won 4-0 on the night with the Os scoring two. I don't know who my Dad went with but he dutifully brought back the programme.

As we had "connections" with the club through Howard's contacts inevitably we had seats near the "celebrities " of the time. Someone who sat behind us on a regular basis was Michael Crawford. He was a massive star of TV at the time before going on to make a name for himself in America. During one game my Dad went up to the bar with him at half time to get a drink. When my Dad returned he was in fits of laughter. When buying the drinks, Michael had asked Dad whether his daughter would like a drink. For those who know me they will be surprised to learn that back in the day I had a head covered in luxuriant curls and the back of my head was all the that Mr Crawford could see. Needless to say I did not share Dad's hilarity as a young lad trying to establish my hormonally charged position in life.

My main memory of 1972 was Dad buying tickets off a tout at about 11.00 on the day of the League Cup final on a relatively deserted Wembley Way. Dad used to get tickets off of the well known "ticket broker" Stan Flashman. A legendary man who apparently sat in the middle of a council flat in a huge armchair surrounded by tickets everyone else wanted but nothing else. You called him and he arranged delivery at a price unless of course you were collecting. Not many did.

We all know what happened that horrible day and I remember little about the day as such, just the game.

I have no idea where we spent the time between the purchase of the ticket and the match, but I do know that I got in the ground which is all that mattered.

We still went to some games, but not that many and I was now old enough to be going on my own.

My next memory is one of the funniest. I had been going to games fairly regularly with mates, but for the game against Liverpool in 1981 we went together and sat in the West Stand. I would have been at University then and this was a bonding experience. We were surrounded by opposition fans with their witty banter as they expected a comfortable win. We were watching the game when from nowhere the much maligned Peter Rhoades Brown broke and galloped towards Ray Clemence. The crowd rose as he approached the goal. He shot, he scored, the crowd went wild. Well almost, I looked round to grab Dad and he seemed to be neither standing or sitting, more of a crouch. It transpires that as he went to get up so he could see what was happening, his raincoat belt buckle got caught in between the rickety wooden seats and he got stuck and missed the goal. That was classic Dad.

I know exactly the last time my Dad went to football. It was in 1985. We were having that great season. We were neck and neck with Manchester City in the race for promotion and we were playing them at home. Just to reassure both my Dad and Chelsea fans in general that whilst we were doing really well some things never changed, we lost 1-0. That however was not why Dad didn't return. In goal for City that day was a guy called Alex Williams. He was a black player. From behind us he was getting barracked racially throughout the game. It was of course unacceptable, but back then it was not unusual even sadly for our own players. My Dad was shocked and very uncomfortable. He never returned and who could blame him.

When I returned from University, I lived near Lords and so cricket was the way I spent time with my Dad. Ironically and somewhat unusually I introduced him to cricket not the other way round. He still supported Chelsea but would watch games with Jamie on TV. I'd take Dad to cricket and rugby but I never asked him again to football. I suspect he would have politely declined.

I never really knew whether he even liked the game or like a lot of Dads whether he did it for me. I suspect that he could have quite easily never gone and he only went because I was obsessed. I never asked him and now I will never know but I have those memories and he'd be pleased that following my beloved Blues has given me such joy and friendships on the way.

IT'S JUST NOT CRICKET…

Pre Season July 2015

The very existence of this article is a lie to the fact that during the closed season break I don't really want to get involved with football. I love my cricket. The Ashes is nearly upon us and I know I will be grumbling like mad when the Community Shield appears and we are in the middle of a test match. I grew up in an era when football stopped and cricket started and the cricket stopped and football started. We had Wimbledon in the middle somewhere but everything was in its place.

As we know, things have moved on. Whilst England were stumbling out of yet another tournament, I read some club has proudly announced they are the first back in preseason training. Our very own CFC is proudly announcing the USA tour is only a month away! Oh please.

When we won the Champions League in 2012, I didn't want the following season to start, basking in the glory was the best ever and I knew when the season started the gloss would fade even a small amount. Little was I to know within 6 months from that glorious night, the most obnoxious little/large man would be at the helm. Anyway I digress; personally I could go football free for another couple of months.

Thing is I do not. Social media pulls you in as do the TV channels. The hype never goes away and then there's that bloody transfer window. The rumours, the fact we are linked with everyone just does my head in. I try to ignore it but fail miserably. The summer so far has been quiet apart from THAT transfer, more of which below.

People are saying we did our business early last year, forgetting that the small matter of the World Cup was going on and so had to be done before players joined up with their squads. With the exception of Liverpool, no one else has made many signings yet

So if I must talk about our beloved Chelsea I will. So what do we know? Well virtually nothing. It appears that we may be buying another knackered striker. I cannot for the life of me see what this is all about. There have to be better options than a player who "may" just pull it off because he's got a year of Premiership bench warming behind him. I have not seen any of the Copa America but even in surroundings familiar to him his performances have been described in similar terms to an ex Liverpool striker now plying his trade in Madrid.

Is this deal a sweetener for something else? Are we lowering Monaco's wage bill in return for one of their young prospects who ripped the Gunners apart at the Emirates? The Mendes factor looms large in this and whilst in Jose I implicitly trust I am going to take a huge amount of convincing.

One of the stars of the Columbian team apparently is

Juan Cuadrado. Really, as I say I have not watched a minute of the Copa, but I would be very happy for him to move on. I did not see anything in what he did last year to convince me that, if heaven forbid Eden or Willian got injured he could step in. Ours is a very competetive league and indeed squad and I cannot see the guy ever competing to that level. I think the Traore work permit may also indicate the departure of Cuadrado.

So the papers are full of us joining the race for Pogba. He looks a potentially stunning player, but personally I would not be happy if Oscar was part of any deal. He is a player with so much skill and potential. There appears from a distance to be a great bond in our squad including Oscar and perhaps I am being naïve in my observation but I hope he stays. A midfield with Pogba and Matic though…. I am so fickle.

With the installation the TFSW at Madrid, the hope of getting the wonderful Varane has all but disappeared (you'd sell him to Liverpool though wouldn't you Rafa?). We do however need quality cover at centre half which I am not convinced would be serviced by shifting Brana over. There has been lots of talk about pushing for John Stones. I would like us to try for him if for nothing else we need to introduce some English guys back in to the team. I know it's a global game but we've lost Frank, Ash and we cannot expect another full season from JT. Hopefully the introduction of RLC to become a more regular member of the squad will assist on that front.

There is certainly a will to introduce the youngsters, but I suspect nothing much will change. Just looking from the outside it doesn't look good for a return for Bamford. I suspect we will not know whether he was actually offered to Newcastle, but good for him if he wants to remain.

One player who does appear on his way out is John Obi. I love the guy but as we know he is probably the player that divides the fans like no other. The bloke in my opinion is class, but as I have said before he suffers from playing in too many games as a holding midfield player when we do not need one. I never understand when we play with two at home, or even any on some occasions. That being said, managers are paid to manage and I am not.

There may also be another departure of a guy who doesn't divide opinion. A man who in simple terms is a club legend and the best goalkeeper the club has had in its history. All this is true but there is just one small problem isn't there and it is where he looks like he is going.

I think there are a couple of things which bother the fans generally. The first is that Arsene couldn't spot a decent keeper if one fell on him. He has continually picked awful keepers, and here is one who is being offered to him on a plate. It just doesn't feel right that we as a club are doing him a favour.

The second thing is the perception if not the reality that we are strengthening a rival. When I watched the Man Utd Arsenal game at the end of the season I was comforted by the fact I thought both teams were at least 4 players short of where we are. So by getting Petr, AFC will improve… but in my opinion it will take a lot more for them to challenge and perhaps even a change in manager.

So, Petr goes with my blessing… especially as it looks like a family driven decision. Ultimately, the club are being unbelievably classy, a fact which will undoubtedly be completely overlooked. I just hope and pray that Thibaut stays fit, because the biggest "told you so" will come from Jose if he doesn't… and we know what the inevitable conclusion from that will be.

Who would I ideally like to come in? As I say, John Stones would be good if we cannot get Varane. I do not think we will get Pogba but ideally I would like Veratti or someone like him. I think we need a little terrier. I sometimes think when a game is drifting; someone to stir things up is required. I think that Cesc has that in him, but not sure he wants to get involved.

One player who I have always wanted is Tevez, another guy who puts himself about. He looked very good for Juve last season and has that "all important Premier League experience". Finally, we will need a backup keeper. People moan about Robert Green, and yes he has a howler in him but all keepers do. He would be fine as a backup, sadly I do not think that either Blackman or Beeney, from what I have seen, are good enough. There's always Hilarious though who still bizarrely seems to be at the club.

Enjoy what's left of the summer break.

REALITY CECH

Community Shield. August 2015

So it has started, the doom the gloom, the general despondency… and yet remind me when the season starts. OK so it was not a meaningless friendly, playing Arsenal can never be that. All the blasé waving away of any significance is, in my opinion, wrong. We all wanted to win if for no other reason than to wind up the graceless nerk who is their manager.

For me the problem wasn't losing, it was the manner of the defeat… a completely limp and ineffectual performance from an almost full strength side. One does not say it often of a Jose team, but Arsenal wanted it more than we did. I think they were at least a week ahead of us in terms of preparation… but I am not entirely sure why.

First let's get the Cech thing out of the way. Well done to all who went and applauded him. He is a true Chelsea legend… but now he's an Arsenal player. The booing of both Cesc and JT allows us the moral high ground. What a farce, why waste your breath, completely childlike although that does a disservice to children. Bottom line is, yesterday he made very little difference as the Arsenal goal was barely under threat. Yes, he will give them more stability, but he was a virtual spectator with the Oscar free kick his sole save… and to be fair I would have been disappointed to have let that in.

But let's concentrate on us. As I said above, I thought we were poor… but had Ray Mears scored that relatively easy chance I suspect we would not have lost. It is beyond irony that Arsenal did to us what we have been doing to them for years. They sat back and hit us on the break. Apart from right at the end when we were chasing the game and offered nothing offensively. In many ways our performance was similar to Jose's first season back when we struggled to break teams down. We did however create two very good chances, and in a couple of weeks' time those sorts of chances will be taken.

It is dangerous to read too much into yesterday, but it is fair to say there were a few causes for concern. I thought that both full backs were average, and the general crossing of the ball from the flanks pretty poor. I did not think that Cesc had one of his better games, but he was man marked. His free kicks and corners were average, but notwithstanding that, he still produced the ball of the game to Falcao who was easily brushed aside.

There are many who are questioning the contribution of both our centre forwards, but to be fair they were not given a sniff. I have seen people slagging off Remy saying it he can't do it in big games. Really? Well for a start yesterday was not a "big" game, and I did not see one opportunity created for him. Yes the number of times he was given offside was disappointing, but he was trying to create an opportunity. The awful Michael Owen in his lamentable BT co-commentary continually slagged him off, but when Falcao made the same mistakes according to Mickey that was because he was trying to create his run.

Yesterday may have been a different story had Eden turned up. He was surprisingly quiet. Stifled by close marking and the usual fouls, he did not appear to get started. Interesting and worrying that without him we looked fairly toothless. The whole attack lacked a presence, and we know what his name is.

On the positive side though, Willian and Matic were both excellent, the two central defenders and the goalkeeper looked solid, and I thought that Oscar and Zouma looked good when they came on although I thought Ray Mears was unlucky to be taken off as he was having a decent game. I think it is safe to say now that Willian is our engine and will now be one of the first names on the team sheet. With all due deference and respect to the wonderful Walter Otton, I do hope we can get a new song for him.

I am however completely mystified by what is happening with the squad. By common consensus, the squad is "thin" and because of the managers insistence on using very few players we visibly tired at the end of the season. So why have there been no additions? I do not think that it's because of the impending stadium move. So what is going on?

If we genuinely have any hopes of competing in the Champions League, we need to add to the squad with more players Jose trusts. I am sure he is a very nice guy, but you are not going to win things by bringing back Victor Moses. For me there are worrying echoes of the season we brought in Sidwell, Ben Haim, and Pizzaro for no money. The time to improve is when you are ahead of your rivals and if nothing else any additions will "freshen" a squad.

All of that being said I saw nothing of Arsenal yesterday which caused me huge concern other than they now have a goalkeeper. The Manchester United spending spree is interesting, but they have no centre forward and no centre half to speak of. Interesting way to build a team, but they have brought in some interesting players. City still have Pellegrini, and Liverpool still have Rogers, nuff said.

We will know a lot more at the end of the transfer window, but I cannot imagine that Jose is "happy" with what's going on. Personally, I do not think that spending £70+million on Pogba is the answer in the same way I do not think that Falcao is the answer (I'm not sure what the question was!) I do think we need back up in attack, and it appears from rumours that we are lining up another left back.

Let us not forget though we are the champions and have the best manager in the modern era… so there is still a lot to be positive about.

AND THE OSCAR GOES TO...

Saturday was great, seeing loads of familiar faces, catching up on summer trips, drinking, gloating about the Ashes... and going back to Stamford Bridge. I also ended up watching a great game of football, albeit not the result that I would have liked.

Having seen the Community Shield, I was slightly wary about what to expect. We looked very sluggish and undercooked. The friendly against Fiorentina did nothing to dispel that thinking, but, as everyone said, the real thing started on Saturday. So it was great that we came out of the blocks so well.

So in no particular order my thoughts are as follows;

• How great was Oscar? He has shown flashes of what he can do since he had been with us which has always been part of the frustration with his recent performances. It is clear he is a class act, and hopefully now he can step up and be that player on a regular basis. I thought he looked our best player until unfairly substituted.

• Following on from that, I was not best pleased when he was taken off on Saturday following the sending off. I don't think many will disagree, Cesc was not having a good game... but he was spared the hook, and it would be great if someone had the guts to ask Jose what his thinking on that was. I can only imagine it's the trust thing, Jose does not yet trust Oscar. He is not, and does not look like being one of Jose's trusted players. It was interesting that when Oscar went off our manager ignored him, but when Cesc was substituted he got the look and the handshake. I am not looking for conspiracies or trouble, but there is no other reasonable explanation for his withdrawal on Saturday.

• The trust thing may also now be hurting the team. I'll talk below about transfers, but the fact that some players have what appears to be no competition for their places is perhaps making them perform at less than 100%. It is very early in the season and so my comments should be taken in that context. It would however have been interesting to see whether Brana would have been on for the second half if we would have had another right or left back on the bench. No one who was at the game will forget poor old Joe Cole and Paulo Ferreira being hauled off after 30 minutes in one game. Our manager is not afraid to take those sorts of decisions, but he does not have the options. Which raises the question as to why no Ake on the bench? There were several poor performances around the pitch, but it was things like misplaced passes and missed tackles which pointed to a lack of fitness.

• When all is said and done, we got a point on Saturday which I would have taken after TC got sent off. For some reason we didn't seem awake at the start of the second half and a very good Swansea side took advantage. I was slightly surprised that the fantastic Montero was substituted and that they didn't go for the win, but all credit to us for the fantastic spirit we produced to hold out and let's be honest dominate for the final 20 minutes, that's why we're Champions.

• I know he cost £8 million, but having Begovic on the bench is very good news. An experienced premier league keeper who "sadly" is already in line for a run in the team. I thought he looked good when he came on and he can certainly cover the hole left by Cech's departure. I have no Hilario/Turnbull-like fears with him taking over from TC at Manchester City on Sunday.

• Fitness aside, I am concerned that we hardly have created a chance for our forwards. Much talk about whether Falcao is going to cut the grade. I cannot think of one clear cut chance he's had. I don't count the shot from the edge of the area on Saturday. The boy Costa looked lively which is good news. As long as he stays fit!

• What of Eden? He missed an easy chance against Arsenal but was otherwise anonymous. Against Swansea he didn't really get going until about 30 minutes from the end. Without him buzzing around we are not the same team. Sadly, when he did get going, he just got kicked. No booking until it was too late.

• One thing which appears to have been missed and not mentioned (I haven't listened to any podcasts yet) was the atmosphere on Saturday. The late kick offs mean that drink may have been taken which always leads to a louder ground normally. I was really encouraged that the MHU was again in fine voice, especially for the last 30 minutes when the team needed us most. The chants of Matthew Harding's Blue and White Army rang out again. I don't know who the guy is who gets it started but he deserves a big pat on the back.

So what about the next game, away to Manchester City? A tough ask but don't we always do something special when least expected? We will have another week of fitness training under our belt. In addition I'm hoping we will have another full back at the club so we can bolster our ranks. It's impossible to know what is going on at the club at the moment but Jose will not want to be 5 points behind City before we have even left August. I have hope that he will again confirm to us why he is the Special One.

You can't just throw money at players and expect things to change. The £27m spent on the hapless Cuadrado proves that but it would be good for everyone's morale if one or two new boys came in. Personally a forward in addition to the full back would be nice, but we shall see.

BLOODY COSTA

Where to start? A poor performance rightly punished by opposition who were principally better than us and deserved to win. There was nothing fake about the result. Yes, from where we were with 15 minutes to go it looked harsh… but on the first half showing, perhaps a true reflection of the game as a whole. That being said, surely credit has to go to our keeper for keeping the score down. A truly heroic performance with the minimum of cover. I thought Matic and Azpi also had solid games, trying to hold things together whilst some or their team mates floundered.

The game went like many recent clashes against City. They dominated the early parts of the game, and we weathered the storm and hung on in there. However badly we played, it's ironic they scored their first and second goals when we were arguably in the ascendancy. I have heard many times over the last 24 hours how many teams will not be able to live with City at Eastlands this season, but to be fair they were playing against a Chelsea team who were nowhere near their best… and let's see how they get on when they are under a bit of pressure.

I do not propose to talk about Citeh that much but suffice to say their recent habit of breaking up play was in full mode. I understand that David Silva committed a game high 5 fouls. He's not exactly Chopper Harris or

Norman Hunter (one for the kids) which means all his fouls were cynical and made to break up play. Was he booked, you can bet your Atkinson he wasn't. The same applied to Fernandhino, 3 cynical fouls before he was booked for his dangerous and reckless challenge on Diego. Straight red, hard to say. But had it been the other way round, Diego would have walked. As for Yaya, WTF does he have to do to get his marching orders? The commentators laughed and said it was probably too late in the game for him to be sent off for his obvious second bookable offence. What? It shouldn't matter. I cannot believe they only committed 19 fouls to our 13. It seemed like double that amount.

All that aside, it's not as if we are not grown up enough to be able to deal with that… but let's just say at our level of performance we needed all the breaks we could get and we got none. Including an offside goal from Ray Mears that wasn't. Has there been a Brazilian footballer with a worst first touch? OK Fred, but apart from him?

It's fair to say he was not alone. Too many of our players are way off their game and the press were quick to jump on the "are they past it" questions about JT and Brana. Let's talk about Brana first. He has had a horrible start to the season. First Montero and then Sterling. Not good for a full back who is not the most mobile. He's looked horribly exposed, and has had little help. In addition he has not been able to cross the ball. Also when overlapping, how many times has he been closed down and his crosses consequently hitting the opposing full backs? This was highlighted even more with our lack of width yesterday. Basically, opposing managers have worked him out, so our manager needs to try something new.

So JT is finished? I don't think so, but I am staggered that he was subbed yesterday. You could have taken Brana or Cahill off just as easily. Why take off your captain? What does they say to the opposition and perhaps more importantly the dressing room? Did Jose really want to give up the result yesterday to make a point he needs more money? Rumours were that JT had something to do with Jose going the first time. Maybe for Casillas read Terry, but who is Jose having an argument with? The players, or up on high? This start of the season has horrible echoes of 2007; I just hope that isn't happening again.

Is it the fault of our defence though? The midfield for me is a bigger worry. The solid shield that was there last year appears to have disappeared. After 2 games we have conceded more on target shots than any other team in the Premier League. Let that sink in. Yesterday we were blown apart in the first 20 minutes or so. There is no point in having Mikel at the club if you are not going to play him. Personally, I would have played him behind Matic and Fabregas and not bothered with Ray Mears. I thought that Cesc was poor in the first half but improved in the second... but what has happened with his free kicks and corners. It was not as if Joe Hart needed catching practice, but that's what he got. We had several free kicks from dangerous positions and produced nothing.

So what is the answer? Probably Paul Pogba, but that is not going to happen... but there needs to be a shake up and a bit of life injected. Not sure Oscar would have played even if he was fit, but hopefully he can play the number 10 that Eden was trying to do yesterday and maybe it's time RLC was introduced in certain games. What we do not need is any more game time for Juan. I keep hearing how great he was in Italy and in the World Cup but for £27 million, it is as bad a bit of business as Nando. At least he looked like a footballer albeit not often enough. This guy has offered nothing from his first calamitous appearance. Yes I want him to succeed, but sometimes things do not work out so let's cut our losses.

We have stopped creating chances. Our shots on target count is not impressive. When Eden missed his golden chance yesterday, it was the first chance from open play we had created since he missed his golden chance against Arsenal in the Community Shield. He is looking off his game. Is it fitness or something else? He seems to be getting little or no help on the creativity front. As I have said before, Willian is the engine... but as much as I like him, he creates very little. It would be good to give our forwards something to go with. Diego had one chance and hit the post.

If truth be told we are really missing Frank's goals. Not the player himself but a player who powers through from midfield to create goals for himself or arrive from nowhere to finish. Yes a player like Frank is hard to replace, but goals from midfield are sadly lacking

So two games, one point… and it looks like we'll be lucky to stay up reading some of the dross on social media. We are a good team with a very good squad and one of the best managers in the modern era. As for anyone calling for Jose to go, are you serious? You get good and bad with him but, I'm happy to take all the bad you can throw at me. There are 91 other clubs in this country who would take him as their manger in a shot not to mention the rest of Europe. Why would you want to get rid of him? Answers on a postcard please? Oh it must be you're desperate for 'Arry or Big Sam to come in and weave their magic? I also read that Jose's father is very unwell. If anyone has been in that awful position you will know how difficult it is to deal with other things around you.

We have not become a bad team with a bad manager overnight. There are problems, but nothing extra fitness and a couple of signings will not sort out. A bit of luck would be good as well!

DUDE. WHERE'S MY TEAM?

I think in the aftermath of Saturday, my biggest annoyance was that I could not enjoy the hilarious results of both Manchester United and Liverpool and the fact that despite our average start to the new season the white half of North London are still not above us in the table (Oh boy has that come back to haunt me).

When the team was announced before the home game against Crystal Palace, I felt that Jose was being Jose. Despite the torrid start to the season that poor old Brana has endured and the fact that he was up against more speedsters meant nothing. Our manager was going to stick with his trusted right back. Our new left back was on the bench so he was obviously fit, but Jose wanted to give Brana another chance.

I admire loyalty, and the reason why Jose has been so successful is that he gets people to run through brick walls for him. It does however get to a stage where this surely becomes unfair on a particular player especially if that player is suffering from a dip in form. Is there something else though, does he not trust Azpi at right back? The formation on Saturday may just have been down to JT's absence and a reluctance to remove even more experience from the back four?

As for the rest of the team, there was little to argue about. That was a team that should have been good enough to beat Crystal Palace. Unfortunately not only did it not beat them it lost to them. So why did it happen? I suppose the simple answer is at least half of the team played poorly or in some cases not at all. In addition, when those are the players who are pivotal, the team is in trouble which at the moment is very much the case.

So let's look at those players who I perceive to be under performing. Brana is not the youngest of guys, he has never been that mobile but this is being targeted. The roasting he got in the first game has now been exposed in the following three games by opposing managers which is in many ways is exacerbating the situation. He played virtually every minute last year and tiredness could be a factor as could be the diminishing defensive cover in front of him. This is not a new problem, but this season it's being highlighted more. It's not clear why he is being hung out to dry at the moment, but we shall have to hope Jose puts him out of his misery albeit temporarily.

The next is Matic. Can anyone point to a single good game he has had since his sending off against Burnley? His influence has lessened. Surely this is not a coincidence. I do not think it's a case of other teams working him out because ultimately it's not that sort of position. So is there any other explanation? It could be that he is simply getting no help and having to cover for other midfield players who are also in somewhat of a trough when it comes to their form. Step forward Cesc. I have no idea whether Oscar is really injured or being held back for the "Pogba deal" but my sincerest hope is he is on his way back and Cesc can be given a rest.

It has defied logic that he has stayed on the pitch the last two games. He is being easily dispossessed, and I think playing to deep. He is better further forward as his lack of pace is cruelly exposed and again he is being targeted. I suspect Jose leaves him on because he is potentially the only one who can play that killer ball through to our forwards. At the beginning of the season I doubted whether Cesc would be in our starting eleven at the end of the season, and nothing has happened to make me change my mind.

We are also seeing Willian being exposed. I do not think he is doing very little different from last season. The major difference however is the players around him are not performing and his lack of a finished product and lack of goals is now being highlighted whereas before it was less of a problem.

On Saturday someone who looked a lot like Eden Hazard was playing for Chelsea… but it was not him. The guy playing on Saturday looked disinterested, sluggish, and generally off the pace. I have no idea what has happened to the real EH, answers on a postcard please.

I think of all our squad he came back from his summer break the least fit. He looked like he had put on a little weight (#notonetotalk) and has struggled to make an impact. Don't get me wrong he has contributed, but has missed chances which he would have converted last year and there is no spark. Against WBA, his work towards the end of the game in protecting the ball and running the clock down was excellent. Indeed, in that game, he played well and his link up play good. It may be that he is just getting really fed up with being kicked every week without much protection. Saturday against Crystal Palace another prime example.

Finally, we have Diego. Against WBA he was magnificent, a real warrior, playing on the edge is what he does and he was in football cliché terms unplayable. Sadly, on Saturday he was back to the moany Diego. Watching him looking for the defender as every high ball was played up to him was dispiriting. He was looking for free kicks rather than the ball and invariably not getting them. His default position appears to be conflict before creativity. I don't know whether there is any truth in the rumours that he is unhappy in London, but there have been too many stories for there not to be something going on.

That being said, when he has his football head on he still looks great. The run he had on Saturday was outstanding, but there was way too little of that. In general there were still too few shots from the team for the keeper to deal with on Saturday particularly in the second half.

We should not however lose sight of how well Palace defended and counter attacked. When all is said and done, they played us very well. In Puncheon they had the best player on the pitch. They had 8 to 10 players behind the ball at all times and it seemed our best chances only came when they had a corner. Bottom line is, we should not be losing at home to them!

So let me end on several positive notes. First the goal. Great to see Falcao scoring. Not only scoring, but a great goal. These were the sort of goals we were scoring regularly last season, crosses in and forwards making for the near post. He looks sharp and presumably he will get a start against Walsall and further starts following Diego's inevitable ban/s.

Then there was the youth. It was great to see RLC with the shackles off. He was bright and powerful. With him and Kenedy on we were running at Palace and causing problems. Albeit they were more tired at that stage of the game, but with these guys on there was a vibrancy I would argue has not been there all season. I really don't get the manager making a point to the owner argument in terms of substitutions. Our manager is a winner. Point scoring over point winning is just not him.

Let me finish by putting Saturday's result into some sort of perspective. My son has been going to the odd couple of matches a season for 6 years and Saturday was the first time he has seen us lose live. Remember, once a blue always a blue. Keep the faith fellow champions.

JM IS STILL THE SPECIAL ONE

September 2015

Let's be fair, for some Chelsea fans of a certain age this is totally unique. They don't understand what's happening as they have never known such a bad start to the season. So their reaction is to do what everyone else does... blame the manager. Change him and we'll be OK. The age of the keyboard fan, the instant knee jerk reactions. Anyone who wants Jose out is in my opinion very wrong. Everyone is entitled to a blip. Some of our players are... so why not the manager?

The man is obviously unhappy. He has looked fed up from the start of the season... and we do know that his father is not very well. Anyone who has been in that unfortunate position will know how difficult it is concentrating on anything else let alone being the manager of one of the biggest football clubs in the world. He is constantly in the limelight and with very little respite from the media. In those circumstances it is sometimes best to do what you can to take your mind off things and maybe that is why Jose is being well, very un Jose?

Some of his recent behaviour is just not him. For a start he is feeling sorry for himself which I have never seen before. To say that Chelsea didn't get what they deserved against Everton on Saturday is just wrong. I am all for defending your team, but we got what we deserved. Nothing! He said we are being punished for every mistake we make, which, whilst accurate, makes him sound like a manager of a newly promoted team not used to the harshness of the Premier League rather than the trophy-laden manager he really is.

He started the season with the public berating of the doctors. Why that wasn't dealt with behind closed doors, who knows? Was it the classic diversion from Jose to take away from not winning our first game? People tend to forget we played the last 30 minutes of that game with 10 men and weren't actually too bad.

Then we went to City. A poor performance, but Jose again insisted it was the wrong result. Not true, but was Jose taking the pressure off the players? He takes JT off at half time and that becomes the story... not the fact we were a poor second best on the day.

This is Jose's biggest managerial challenge. One can only imagine the pressures of managing Real Madrid, but at the moment, from the outside looking in, he seems to be unable to motivate the players or change games. This is the biggest surprise as it has always been a massive strength. Yes we have played against teams who have upped their game from last season, but with all due deference and respect we are speaking about Swansea (who lost to a 10 man Watford on Saturday), Palace, and Everton. These are teams we should be beating, certainly the first two at home.

If Jose is sulking because of the poor transfer window, he should stop and work with what looks to me like a decent squad. I think his continuing faith in Brana who is obviously struggling is losing him a lot of love. Fans can simply not understand why an obvious weakness is not being addressed. I can fully understand why things were not changed last season, and it is unfortunate that we lost Luis without ever seeing the best of him. So we buy another £20m plus left back in Baba Rahman who has sat on the bench and was nowhere to be seen on Saturday. I do not think he is injured but may get a run out in the League Cup.

I appreciate that there are a million factors behind the scenes we do not know about, but unless Baba was not wanted by Jose... his non-appearance is strange.

The injury to Oscar is a major factor to our current problems. He looked very good in the first game against Swansea and because of the sending off was substituted. A fit Oscar would surely mean the dropping of Fabregas or pushing him further forward. The manager cannot be blamed for injuries, but where is our plan B. We have a good squad and with 30 plus players on loan we should not be short of options.

There has been a lot of talk that our slow start to the season was down to lack of fitness and the commercially driven air miles gathering in Australia and the States. That cannot have helped but the season is now over a month old and the squad's fitness should be there by now. There is still however no speed of thought or actions. Just think back 12 months ago to the goal against Burnley. All one touch passes and a decisive finish. We are a million miles from that.

Whilst the defeat against Everton was a poor performance from both our defence and midfield, let's not kid ourselves... our attack is equally bad. There were very few chances created, and virtually no shots on target which is becoming a bit of a theme. There is the constant fannying about outside the box not shooting and the distribution from the flanks is woeful. These are basics.

Can you blame the manager for players who haven't turned up this year? Our game changer is Hazard and there is something seriously wrong with him. So why is a manager who previously was not averse to substituting under performers within 30 minutes of kick off in some games constantly picking players who by their very own high standards have just not turned up this season? Lack of options perhaps? As a team they need to start playing for the shirt.

Many people gave Jose grief for introducing Kenedy on Saturday. It has to be said he wasn't great, but I think it was a good move. We are far too predictable, and he offers something different. He is young and inexperienced and needs to be given time. I am hoping he starts in the League Cup, but it's unlikely I suspect. We are in transition and the gradual introduction of Zouma is to be commended, but his positional naivety certainly added to our woes on

Saturday. That being said, he is learning on the job and that can only be good.

So where do we go from here? A lot depends on the next two games and a certain Russian. We should be too strong for Maccabi in the Champions league. I am all for playing a strong side to gain some momentum taking us into the game against Arsenal on Saturday. More conflict in store for Jose when he meets Arsene. More absolute tripe about shaking hands and all ultimately an irrelevance in what will be a massive game for Jose and the club.

I am hoping that some of our players will step up for that one and start getting angry. If Coquelin kicks one of ours, kick him back harder! If Jose is struggling with other issues, surely the team need to start fighting for him before it is too late. Obviously we have one player who is constantly fighting, but sadly to no great effect at the moment. We also have a huge part to play and we need to create a big atmosphere. Let's save any big love for Petr until after the final whistle.

It is a broken record, but older fans need to remind younger fans that there is no divine right to success. The last 15 or so years have been amazing, but nothing should be taken for granted. Sport is cyclical and no one dominates for ever, but do not think getting rid of the best manager the club has ever had will make things any better.

BILLY SMART'S 1 CHELSEA 0

I suppose it's partly my fault and partly yours. If it hadn't been for people like me paying my subscriptions we wouldn't be in the state we are in would we? This weekend, and the reaction to Diego Costa, has been everything that is wrong with modern football.

So where to start? A derby game and the hype begins with the playground antics of the respective managers. Will they or won't they shake hands. Who cares? What has that go to do with anything? Press conferences used to be for the written press and we'd read about it later or on Ceefax or ring up Club Call. The banality of the questioning is beyond belief. It's no wonder Jose always looks so bloody miserable.

We then have a 12.45 kick off. Personally, I don't like them. I had just about got used to 4.00 on a Sunday and the occasional Monday nighter, but this and the 5.30 are only enjoyable when my team is involved. The only solace is that if we are on at 5.30 at home I can avoid 3-piece-Redknapp. He really is annoying.

So to the game. We have a London derby and so there should be blood and thunder. We don't like them… and they don't like us. Just like it should be. There should be bad tackles and fouls. The players should care, and pride is at stake. Derby games are rarely things of beauty, but they should make the heart race for the fans.

So on Saturday there was not one bad foul. There were a couple of misplaced challenges due to bad timings, but there was not one thing that happened that could in any way be described as either reckless or dangerous. The game last year contained a couple of leg break tackles and an unpunished punch to the head. There was not one tackle last Saturday that could have injured anyone.

That however doesn't work for the media. This was the "Battle of Stamford Bridge". Really? No it was a badly refereed game with 2 sending offs and lots of fuss about nothing. Some pushing and shoving and some Billy Smart Clown dives. All that was missing was a Charlie Carolli and a clown car with the doors falling off, which we sort of had when the Arse imploded.

It seems that Diego continues to be demonised and hung out to dry just as he was last season. I am no apologist for him because he is an annoying player who must be horrible to play against… but he is our annoying player that every single one of the 91 other clubs would love to have him fighting for their club. What physical damage has he done to anyone? Contrast that with the challenge on him by Fernandhino.

When Diego arrived, he came with a reputation. He'd already shown us when he played for Atletico what a handful he was, and he wound us up when they won at the Bridge. Unfortunately, the referees in this country did not give him a chance. They just perceived what he was all about and that was that. When he was booked for a dive in his first game at Burnley, he looked like he wanted to cry. We all did Diego. A dreadful decision, a clear penalty and sending off for the goalkeeper... but no it had to be some dark deed by the new boy according to Mr Oliver.

He is no angel, and a lot of his antics deserve bookings... but then we got the ridiculous witch hunt driven by Sky after the League Cup semi-final against Liverpool. The stamp, possibly intentional who knows, and a three match ban followed. The hype ramped by Sky running the headline "Costa crimes". What an absolute farce, but they pay the money and, as proved at the weekend, together with BT, they now run football and there is nothing you or I can do about it.

I found it quite interesting that in the storm that followed, most of the ex-pros were reluctant to slag Costa off. Each of them would have loved to have him in their team. Sadly for us I cannot see him staying past this season. Why should he? He's been vilified since day one and he has every right to think our league is officiated by clowns and run by jokers.

We then had the pitiful whingeing of Arsene. He called Costa a disgrace and said he is allowed to get away with everything? Absolutely correct you hypocrite. At Palace not a month ago one of his players committed enough fouls for two sendings off. So much so he had to substitute him. He wasn't complaining then was he? Yes, defend your own team... but leave us alone.

I've heard it asked what the difference between waving

an imaginary card is and what Wenger said? I honestly don't know. Personally I could do without both. Why is he not thanking Diego? All people are talking about post game is that instead of the fact that he is the only manager this season who has come up short against us. He didn't target Brana... or the crowd... or Cesc. He's so predictable... to the point of arrogance. If I was an Arsenal fan that's what I would be livid about.

All of this has then been followed up by the appropriately titled FA. Their rulings against this club have now reached farcical proportions. No consistency, no logic and the backbone of a jelly fish. Would they have done anything had Arsene said nothing and the media just analysed the football? Perhaps Jose should have shouted louder when Fernandhino got away with battering Diego?

HYPOCRISY

Its official I am a hypocrite. I know it to be true.

Let me set a hypothetical scenario. We are managed by let's say an ex Liverpool manager who just happens to be Spanish and bears a stunning resemblance to a person in the catering trade. This manager has been rude about us before he joined and when appointed our manager refused to discuss/apologise. Let's just say that he drops one of our favourite players but the people he puts in are no better and he keeps picking two underperforming players who in the case of certainly one of them is stinking the place out.

What do you think would be the greeting for that manager would be on Saturday? Personally in that hypothetical scenario I would be livid and not a happy bunny. I would be questioning whether he knew what he was doing especially when he again picks the aforementioned two players.

Some of you may have guessed where I am going with this! What has happened to my Jose? Where is he? Why is he choosing to ignore what appears on the face of it to be obvious to the rest of us?

Is there something going on behind the scenes that none of us are aware of? There can be no other logical explanation for either the strange selections, or the lack of passion of some of the performances. The one thing you could always say about Jose's teams is that is exactly what they were. A team. On Wednesday there seemed to be an element of waiting for something to happen rather than anyone taking the game by the scruff of the neck. Watching defenders bring the ball out and finding no one to pass to was disheartening. Against Porto we were half decent but got kicked to pieces and had a stonewall penalty turned down. Yet again we looked second rate again in defence.

We no longer have any leaders on the pitch, but worse still we have one sitting unused on the bench. I do not watch John Terry in training. I do not know if he's lost something, but I do know that he could not possibly do any worse than what is out there. I think that since his brush with the media he has certainly become less rabble-rousing when playing… but with a new keeper and centre back there needs to be an authoritive figure out there. It is years since we have been so disorganised at the back.

Personally, I think Jose is trying to settle on a back four and stick with it and that is why those four are likely to play again on Saturday. It appears for the second season in a row a decent left back will sit on the bench whilst our best right back plays at left back. This year is slightly more understandable with Baba being younger, but in relative terms could he be any worse than Brana is at the moment if introduced with Azpi swapping?

For the record, I love Jose. He is the best manager we have ever had and ever likely to have. He has more credit in the bank than anyone else. I do not want him going anywhere and if he has to have one bad season to get it out of his system then so be it. I can live with that… but will Roman? The fact he is still in a job after the season we are having it looks like maybe there are a few issues behind the scenes which we are not aware of… not least the illness to Jose's father.

All that being said, the continuation with Brana and to a lesser extent Cesc make no sense. Of course he can see that Brana is being targeted by opposition coaches (except Arsene) but chooses to do nothing to address that. He has not become a bad manager overnight, but if you looked at that team in the last two games in isolation you could argue that they were not playing for the manager.

I saw no fight against Newcastle until we scored. Yes it was a good comeback, but we got back in the game without displaying tactical acumen although of course there has to be spirit to get a draw from a 2-0 deficit.

Also, why leave players at home on a European trip if they are not injured? It's not as if we are hard up and saving on air fare and accommodation. How can that do anything but harm team unity? I don't believe everything I read in the press, but there has to be a certain amount of truth in those stories

All that said, on Saturday I shall support the team as I always do. I will grumble in the pub beforehand that I cannot believe Brana and Cesc are both playing and JT is on the bench. When in the ground I will not chant against the manager but I will have a secret prayer that he has rediscovered his mojo, that things are good in his world, and he can again make us champions (I'd settle for competitive at the moment) because "In Jose We Trust".

TO TWEET OR NOT TO TWEET?

October/November 2015

I was on holiday recently and the hotel didn't have free WIFI. I went to reception and found out you could buy it but you couldn't use it on two devices at the same time. I said that was crazy and the receptionist, after blaming the provider, said, "but nobody's forcing you to use it!"

His answer for someone in the service industry was rude but prophetically spot on in terms of my current reading of the press and social media.

I have really embraced Twitter. It has been a conduit for new friends, the birth of my blogging and podding "careers" and now this book (yes it's Twitter's fault!) a great source of information about the arts music and books but at the moment it's a difficult read.

Last Saturday night whilst the X Factor was droning on in the background I saw a Tweet from the Times journalist Oliver Kay saying that Jose had collapsed in his hotel room and had been rushed to hospital. I immediately went on to the BBC website and saw nothing. There was no other mention and upon further inspection "Oliver Kay" was an imposter and the tweet just mischief.

What the f#ck possesses some loser to do that. Taking away football rivalries for a second this really makes no sense on any level. Going to the trouble of replicating a journalist's account and tweeting shite. Thankfully I cannot get into the head of the saddo. I suppose it beats having to do your geography home work.

As we know football is all about opinions and there may well be a faction of "fans" who would like us to get rid of our manager. Step forward the @Mourhinooutclub account on Twitter. Divisive drivel with the inevitable threat to fly a plane with the banner etc. Whether it's a Chelsea fan, who knows? But as I have mentioned before, I'd rather lose the players than the manager.

Twitter also links in to all the headline stories from the newspapers. Every day there is something new from Hans Christian Anderson school of journalism. The club are doing this, the cardboard box for desk clearing has arrived, and the players have turned up for training with pitchforks and lighted torches.

I know it is their job, but why are the press hounding Jose out of British football? Taking my Chelsea hat off, surely his presence here has to be in their interest. Every day however there is some sensationalist crap about his last chance... the dressing room has been lost, and the owner is just about to pull the trigger.

There are a few out there writing good stuff such as Dominic Fifield, a journo who seems to have some inkling about what is actually happening. The latest however is the hijacking of a piece from the cfcuk fanzine by the Sun. Written before the proverbial hit the fan. On the whole, a positive piece which rightly questioned Jose's comments on our away fans. Used without consent, and another stick to beat the man with.

It is hard to remember a more collective effort from our press to vilify a manager. It is fair to say that Jose sometimes does not help himself. The whole Eva episode hangs heavy. It is impossible to know what impact that had on the internal moral at the club. I have always said with Jose you take the good with the bad.

Maybe the press are continuing the assault because they know other fans are desperate for him to go and hopefully end up at their club!

The bottom line is no one knows what Roman thinks. He will undoubtedly be unhappy as this is the worst the club has done during his ownership. He probably knows that getting Hiddink in for 6 months will "rescue" the season and maybe get us into the top four but then what?

It is obvious that there is something wrong at the club. From lack of fitness, to some stellar players stinking the place out. It is true that Jose tried to get players in in the summer, and I have no doubt that the addition to the squad of say Stones and Pogba would have given a bounce effect to the team and certainly would have changed some results. It didn't happen for whatever reason, and we have to hold on until January. The really interesting question is whether Jose will still be there?

If he is, then for me it proves the club let him down in the summer. An admission that the additional players Jose wanted was the right way to go. The alternative is not worth thinking about. I, like many, recall when we heard he'd gone first time round. It was like being chucked when you were circa 15/16 years old by the "one". Your stomach churned, a feeling of helplessness knowing nothing you can do will change things. It pervades your thoughts and makes you miserable!

Despite the defeat at Stoke the team showed more fight and whilst not playing brilliantly the most recent performances show an improvement. The luck however continues to elude us. Another appalling referee which Jose cannot even speak about! Stoke didn't even lose that many players to the respective squads during the Rugby World Cup!

For Charlie Adams read Diego Costa and "that" tackle gets 24/7 coverage from Sky. Whilst a persecution complex is never good, it is sometimes difficult to reconcile the treatment afforded to our club compared with others. I saw footage of McClaren coming on to the pitch at half time after they got the wrong end of a penalty decision and wagging his finger at the referee. What I do not see is the admonishment from the FA and his subsequent fine/ban.

So does this mean? I will not look at Twitter or the press, what do you think?

THE GOOD, THE BAD AND DIEGO

November 2015

Taking into account our start to the season, I sat myself down on the sofa for Sunday's game against Spurs expecting to be watching the game through my fingers. There were however two factors which I thought might be in our favour. The first was their journey overseas on Thursday, and second the deluded chat of them winning the league following their demolition of West Ham last weekend. They always do that. Just like their north London neighbours who, with alarming predictability, have an injury crisis having not strengthened their squad but frankly who cares.

Our season has pretty much been a nightmare so I had no idea what to expect, although following Diego's MIA performances and Norwich and Maccabi I had thought we might start with a false number 9 and so it proved. Following JT's injury, our defence picked itself and I for one was really pleased to see Oscar in the team. He rarely gets picked for tough away games.

The start was encouraging save for Cesc's picking out white shirts with every pass. It was interesting to see that we were being paid a great deal of respect despite our lowly position. For all the joy at winning back to back games, the reality was we were pretty average in both against poor opposition… but winning breeds confidence. There was far less nervousness in our play. They came closest to scoring in the first half albeit most of their shots came from outside of the box and the Hurrykane didn't get a sniff. For all our moans about introducing youth, Kurt is quietly becoming a real rock at the back.

The second half was interesting for the fact that both teams cancelled each other out. Before the game, I was informed that from both sets of outfield players this season we had been outscored 15 goals to 6… yet I can't remember Asmir having anything to do in the second half. The save of the match came half way through the half from Eden who cannot buy a goal at the moment. So in general there was a feel good factor after the game and we'd earned a point with our third clean sheet in a week. Yes we all know a point is not really good enough but certainly it was one more than most predicted and I suspect one more than most teams will get there this season.

There is however a slightly bitter taste. We approached the game like most "lesser" teams do when they come to the Bridge. Denying the space, harrying and closing down with the hope of hitting on the break. Our whole attitude was about preserving what we had.

For me the positives are the fact that this was probably the most disciplined performance of the season with the implication that the players are once again listening to the manager. I do however feel we are some way off of what I would call the "modern" way of playing. On Saturday I watched MOTD. Basically because I had nothing better to do and it's always good to gloat at another team doing worse than we are. Step forward Mr McLaren's boys. As I watched Palace tear them apart I looked at their quick wing men and thought we do not currently have that pace and power to do that. The irony being this is exactly how Jose likes his teams to play.

We do however have Kenedy and we have Traore neither of which will be risked to any great extent for so long as we are in the position we are. It will be interesting if Kenedy is again given the full back role against Bournemouth they are similar opposition to Norwich so perhaps similar tactics. I'd also like to see RLC given a run out. Despite having a vastly improved game in terms of effort and commitment Cesc slows us down and with the importance of Porto, maybe he'll be rested?

Before I go on to discuss the invisible man, I just want to big up Asmir. Following Carlo's departure, for years we had awful back up keepers. Then we signed Mark Schwarzer. He turned out to be an incredibly shrewd purchase but Begovic is even better. There are those who have pointed out some goals conceded in his run of games would have been saved by Thibaut. It's an argument that is impossible to settle. The bottom line is he hasn't let us down, and again on Sunday I thought he was solid and in the first half made some crucial saves albeit ones you would expect him to make. So if Thibaut is back this weekend, thank you Asmir.

So what is going on with Diego? His performances against Norwich and Maccabi were anonymous. Yes he scored the winner against Norwich, but he could and should have had a hat trick in the first half. Last season he was the anti-Torres and now he's a copy-Torres. Slightly harsh on the basis he took his goal superbly, but the rest of the time he was hiding on the wing rather than terrorising defenders in the box as he was this time 12 months ago. He, like the rest of the team, appears to be suffering from a crisis of confidence. Just think back to the brilliant hat trick he scored against Swansea last season. He created panic in their back four and was poaching in the box.

Now he cuts a lonely figure. He didn't battle in those two games, but perhaps that is the problem... the ridiculous reaction to a tough old style centre forward seems to have taken its toll. He is his own worst enemy, but he has been subject to ridiculous bans and hypocritical treatment from refs and he's probably a bit fed up with it all. Against Norwich however there was however a throwback to the time the crowd finally got fed up with Didier's antics and let him know. When Costa went down when he should have stayed on his feet I think he would have known what the general feeling was. He didn't get blatant penalties last season so I'm not sure why he thinks he would get them this year for far less. It was interesting that for the first time the crowd got on his back but were not specifically having a go at him. On the two more obvious occasions in the Norwich game when the ball was played into the box and there was no one within a mile of the ball there was a groo, a cross between a groan and a boo.

Had he been arsed, he surely would have scored against Maccabi but it appeared he couldn't be bothered despite the kiss and cuddle he got from Jose at half time. On Sunday on the bench against Spurs his behaviour was childish and disrespectful to his manager, team mates and the fans. It's not about being dropped. From my point of view he looks like he just doesn't want to be here anymore and he doesn't care if he annoys and upsets. The fact that he showed blatant disregard for everything at the weekend, and the club are not fining him, says to me he's off and maybe even in January. According to the reaction I got on Twitter, not many agree. I think he'll go back to Madrid with perhaps one of their players coming back the other way. There was an excellent article by Graham Souness in the Sunday Times which speculated that he has been worked out by defences and is therefore less effective. Whatever the reason, something is not right and at the moment it looks irretrievable. A great shame.

So hopefully another couple of wins against Bournemouth and Porto and the momentum will build before we reacquaint ourselves with the Tinkerman. Another team, like Palace, full of pace and goals. Hopefully by then we will be well on our way back to discovering our mojo and we can comfort ourselves with the fact that we know what damage Claudio can do, to his own team (not exactly my best prediction)!

THE CHALLENGES AHEAD

As fans, we have taken more abuse than most since the arrival of Roman. We have certainly taken over from Manchester United in this regard. We are, in no particular order, plastic, we are either chavs or chavskis, we are Johnny come latelys, and… we should also not forget we are also accused of being racist.

It is very interesting how this has evolved, and yet the likes of Manchester City following the influx of their money have only really received abuse from not selling out the Etihad. Personally, I have no problem with Citeh. Their fans have always been decent with us and their support in what was the old 3rd Division was brilliant.

We know that a lot of the cause of much of the abuse we get is jealousy. We have wound up a lot of opposition fans with our success notwithstanding that some of the main culprits choose not to look at how much their respective clubs have spent in recent years. At least 3 of those teams play in red. The other lot that play in white and navy seem just bitter.

It's strange how Chelsea fans never seem to get credit for continually selling out our league games and more so our cup games in all competitions.* I know we haven't got the biggest ground, but even so our support is consistent. We got vilified for the abuse we gave Rafa Benitez, but it's apparently OK for other teams to hound their managers out.

I have no idea whether Jose will still be at the club by the time you read this (I sincerely hope he is), but the support he has received has been nothing short of spectacular. Let's face it, it's not hard. We know he's the best, and losing him would be self-defeating. Even so to show such a united front to the rest of the football world is something to be proud of.

I do however think we are not far away from one of our biggest challenges as fans, Wembley. When we eventually leave the Bridge, albeit temporarily, it appears our new home will be there.

Over the last couple of years, to pay for the stadium, the FA have successfully managed to erode what was the magic of going to Wembley. There was no finer day out than the FA Cup final. We all accept the game has moved on and many clubs have devalued that particular competition, but by having the semi-finals there the FA done most of the damage themselves.

I appreciate the club have very few options, but playing our home games at Wembley for what I can only imagine will be at least three years is going to be very tough on us as fans. Any Wembley final that follows will inevitably be not be as special. That however I believe will be the least of our problems.

Some will remember when Arsenal played their champions league games there. They didn't do well at all. We know now they just don't do well generally in that competition, but that was difficult for them and a real lift for their opposition. Generating atmosphere in what will be on most occasions an almost half empty stadium will be a massive challenge.

One of the main reasons for our upturn in fortunes from the 90s onwards was the redevelopment of the Bridge and getting rid of the running track. Before that happened it was much more difficult to produce an intimidating atmosphere for really big games especially midweek. That horrible sight of the opposition scoring in the last 10 minutes of a game and the scorer running to their fans over that running track still puts me in a cold sweat. Once the ground "closed in", opposition players were much more intimidated and subsequently we started winning those important games.

Most "bigger "clubs fans are accused of being quiet at home games. All seater stadia and the price of tickets have been the main cause of this. There is also an inevitability of the more successful clubs fans getting used to winning and only being really up for the more important games. Remember the chant of "60,000 muppets" at Old Trafford?

I hope that something can be arranged with the club so that this can be addressed and all efforts done to encourage a decent atmosphere. The liaison with the fans and the Chelsea Supporters Trust will be essential, but ultimately it's up to us to generate the atmosphere as best we can… win or lose. Let's not forget the players will have their part to play in generating excitement.

For me and many others, the match day is a very social experience. Whether it be a visit to the cfcuk stall or the pub… or a restaurant, the chance to catch up with friends is all part of the day. I think that it will take a time for fans to find their feet in setting out their routine. Those who know the area well are aware it's not Chelsea in more ways than one!

Apart from the lousy transport links, regular attendees will hope that the local hostelries will up their game. There may be a lot more people drinking in the stadium which will definitely be a loss to the day. Subject to the weather, I would hope that stalls on the exterior concourse could be set up… but we all know against certain opposition the chances of trouble will sadly prevent this.

For me, it will be up to the Trust, the Club and fans to make this work. It's a big ask but the reward at the end of the lodging period will be huge. An amazing state of the art stadium still in Chelsea and still at our home Stamford Bridge. The club may lose some fans but gain others. Sensible pricing at such a huge venue could encourage the return of younger fans and I hope that opportunity is taken.

It will be tough, but we as Chelsea fans will be up for the challenge.

*Indeed we had the highest attendance percentage of the season during a particularly bad season

THE LONG GOODBYE

December 2015

It was inevitable wasn't it? Despite the length of time it took, and the hoping and praying that things had changed he's gone.

Many wrote eloquently and passionately within the 24 hours of his departure. Personally, I wanted to see how I felt after giving it some time. Well the question was answered outside Hamleys on the Sunday before Christmas. I fell hook line and sinker for a fake Twitter post from someone purporting to be Duncan Castle of the Times. It said LVG out TSO in. My stomach lurched. I felt sick, but thought good for him and we as a club get everything that's coming to us. Whilst I think anyone who pretends to be a journo needs some kind of help, the scenario does have a very plausible ring to it and I suspect it's only a matter of time before it happens.

I have read that Roman didn't want to sack Jose, and took the decision reluctantly. I'm sorry, but if he didn't want to… he didn't have to. To then see one of his trusted advisors explaining that there was "palpable discord" between the players and a person whose name he couldn't utter was stunning in its lack of respect and sensitivity to the greatest manager the club has ever had. I am not naïve. I understand he is just a mouthpiece, but any of the stuff I have read about this particular mouthpiece having any influence on whether TSO stayed or went fills me with absolute horror. What are his credentials against a man who has won everything in football management?

Let's be honest, this season has been poor. One of the worst for a generation. It has been painful watching the temporary demise of a man the vast majority of Chelsea fans love. Everything he tried failed. The players were no longer listening to him. A man who had complete control and shepherded a limping horse over the line last season had apparently lost the dressing room. What had he done to alienate players who were gallivanting round the pitch with him, having helped them to, in many cases, their first piece of silverware?

Many point to Evagate. There is no question it didn't help. It seems completely irrational that this incident set the whole playing staff against him. It is probably a point where many of the players questioned him as a person they wanted to play for. If the equivalent would have happened in your place of work/study/social surroundings you would forever look at that person in a different light. An apology or an acceptance of doing wrong would have helped. It was out there, but an act of contrition may have gone some way to perhaps making things better.

The point however was that we had been awful in pre-season and the Community Shield which all happened before Evagate. Players weren't fit and had travelled more miles than Judith Chambers (one more for the kids) before the season started. Another leader in the dressing was let go despite the manager's wishes (a massive loss for TSO to stomach). Players on the shopping list didn't come as our bids were too late and too slow and our signings with the exception of Begovic and Pedro were both pointless and embarrassing. Why wasn't he backed in the transfer market? All this and many rivals and non-rivals having worked out how to stop us playing should have been a massive warning to those in charge. Was he not sacked earlier than he was because the club accepted some of the responsibility for the position we were in?

All of that doesn't really explain why some players simply stopped trying. Perhaps the players had had enough of the public beratings. Maybe they were fed up with seeing mediocre performances by some individuals being rewarded with a certain place in the team. Maybe the players were fed up with his name being chanted to the exclusion of theirs. Jealous that they weren't getting the same adulation?

None of this however excuses them not giving 100% for us the fans. Watching against Sunderland as Brana was chasing and harrying and assuming responsibility, or watching Diego making forward runs and pointing to where he wanted the ball was laughable. The crowd aren't stupid and the players got it in the neck but to watch them play like they had been freed of some curse was an interesting indictment of how we have been playing.

Many fans, me included, were perplexed at TSO's

continued reluctance to use young players. I think we can all agree that when you are desperate for wins the last place you would look would be untried kids. No one however can tell me that some of the lads we have could have done any worse than what was out there... not to mention the legion of talented kids parked elsewhere. The treatment and hot air spouted about RLC by TSO was a case in point. "He is ready. " "He will have a run in the team." Etc. He got 45 minutes and a public coating how did that help? If any of these things change, then we will get a better insight into why a prize asset has been let go for the second time.

The club's reluctance to stick with a proven winner over a bunch of individuals who downed tools is baffling. Yes I am a hypocrite because this is exactly what happened to AVB, but that only happened after they realised he was just not up to it. With TSO, the club knew what they were taking back. You get trophies, charm, aggravation, embarrassment, passion, and more trophies. None of what's happened can be a surprise, so why set him adrift now? Why did he not get the loyalty awarded to other less deserving of such treatment? Why did the club always leave him out to dry? Why was he always battling when he was trying to protect the club from shocking officiating, ridiculous fines and stadium bans?

The owner spoke to the players after TSO had gone, just like he did after AVB left saying he didn't want to sack the coach but now the players need to react. Why didn't he make the speech before? Maybe TSO didn't want him to, but, according to one paper, the request was made the day before he was sacked. A last request from a condemned man. A "dead" season to rebuild under him wasted.

He really is a Special One. I will have nothing but love and respect for the man. Of course I have never met him, but when he said he was one of us I believed him. He leaves behind a trail of broken hearts wherever he's been. His name was even chanted at a Real Madrid basketball game. Fans know.

So with a heavy heart I say good bye again with the thought that the players are replaceable but he is not. Thank you Jose.

SPINELESS

January 2016

When I started writing this I intended it as a criticism of the club's forward planning and not doing their best to replace what was an astonishing spine but it's not turned out like that. Everyone has vented their anger at the club in the last couple of months following the departure of the man who caused the "palpable discord" but I think it's time we had a proper look... and what a mess we are in. I'm not specifically talking about our league position but the disarray of the playing staff and the mountains which need to be climbed to get back to where we were even pre-supposing we can.

The team has lost its spine and its leaders. We no longer can call upon Cech, Terry, Lampard and Drogba to be that spine so let's take a look at the forward planning to deal with that fact. At first look it appears that we have been negligent in that regard but that may not quite be the case. There is also the caveat that there are not many leaders out there. Perhaps they have to be grown from within?

They have replaced Cech with a worthy successor. Thibaut has had his critics, mostly because he is not Cech, but he is young, and, in my opinion, will be a worthy successor to Cech if he remains at the club.

What about the centre half. Let's start by saying that JT is irreplaceable for many reasons. The only youth product to break into the team in a decade plus and a leader of men so let's not be too hard in saying he hasn't been replaced. The club brought in Gary Cahill who is a more than decent defender but is not quite there. We can all see the potential of young Kurt and it is to be hoped he will be that replacement, but he isn't yet. I think Tomas Kalas has suffered by his stunning performance away to Liverpool which will be remembered for one thing only. He did look class, but has been shipped out so there is no chance to know whether if he ever comes back that position can be his. A starting back four including both Zouma and Kalas is unlikely, but the club has tried to plan ahead. It is more likely that Andreas Christensen will be the one if he wants to come back.

I think midfield is where we have the biggest hole to fill. One thing which has been massively clear is that you cannot replace a player like Frank Lampard. My issue is notwithstanding his greatness and the success we had with him playing in a certain role, we have never tried to replace him with a similar player. All our midfielders have been small or slight, all being prepared for the arrival of Pep which never happened. No one can dispute the industry and skill of Willian, nor can the club be blamed for the inexplicable demise of Matic... but the sale of De Bruyne looks madness. As with Romelu, the money was too good to be turned down but there was no thought of succession.

The general feeling was his attitude stunk. Well that's an interesting perception now looking at all the knives that were inserted in Jose's back by various players who simply downed tools.

The club had bought a successor to Drogba but sold him. There has been much debate about Lukaku but there can be no arguing with his scoring record which let us not forget is for a team outside the top four. At the time the money received looked fantastic business but in hindsight it may not have been. His replacement was less money and went some way to winning the league for us in 2014/2015, but his purchase should have also been backed up with a younger striker to learn and fit in whenever Diego was having one of his numerous breaks. The Special One was not so special in letting him go unless he was told you can't have Diego without selling Lukaku... which is perfectly plausible. As we know Remy hasn't been given a chance, but he was never going to be anything other than a squad member as opposed to a first teamer. At the moment we are woefully lacking in that department. I know some will say Lukaku never looks good against us and I think perhaps naively that's because he's a fan. He didn't celebrate any of Everton's goals wildly on in the 3-3 home draw and was quiet throughout.

Hindsight is wonderful but both Lukaku and De Bruyne would walk into our team at the moment and some of the blame has to be laid at the manager's door subject to whatever financial constraints he was under. The club should not however get away scot free. Why is it that in each of the three seasons following championships we have failed to go out into the transfer market properly and back the manager? We have ended up with the likes of Sidwell, Pizarro, Ben Haim... and this year another left back not getting a look in and Hector, Papasmurf etc.

So can we construct a new spine? As I have said, we have Courtois and Zouma. We have RLC and Costa or maybe someone else. Is that something that can be built on? The next 5 months will be very interesting. If we are not getting top four and we are not going down... should we play the youth. I am one of those beating that particular drum and feeling much maligned. Against Scunthorpe we chose to play Azpi when he had a broken cheek bone and left Baba on the bench. Surely he cannot be that bad that he was going to be terrorised by a 4th tier forward. Also Pedro was picked ahead of Kenedy in the same game. Why? Having rested Pedro he may not have played so badly against the baggies? This is not a management which will "play the youth" despite what is being said. Two half time appearances for RLC and Kenedy is not a revolution.

It is an interesting debate as to whether we as a club would accept a season with no trophies to bring through a couple of youth players as first team regulars. I think the answer is a resounding no. Watching the Albion game when every single misplaced pass was greeted with a groan was disheartening. Players are not allowed to make mistakes. Young players by their very nature make mistakes, but without giving them game time we will never know whether they can hack it. Players like Dele Alli will make mistakes but he will learn by them. So let us see RLC for the rest of the season, and let's not groan if and when he screws up. If at the end of the day he's not good enough so be it but at least we will know.

Presumably whichever new manager turns up will look to bring in new players and any chances for the youngsters will dissipate. The continual change in managers means that there can never be any continuity for the youth and consequently there will be a lack of trust. Ultimately a young manager is needed who is given a brief to introduce a young side whilst removing the old guard. Someone like AVB perhaps, but remind how that worked out.

REASONS TO BE CHEERFUL?

So Arsenal are defeated and everything is right in the world. Well not quite, but it certainly looks better than it did. Ironically, before the game at the Emirates, I compiled a list of reasons to be cheerful principally because I wasn't. So here am being positive with apologies for the sound of a barrel being scraped towards the end.

1. We are undefeated under new management. Not to be sniffed at. I understand we have the longest unbeaten streak of any team in the Premier League at the moment which I find staggering but there you go. I think it says more about the Premier League than it does about us. We are hardly taking the league by storm but to come back from 2-0 down against Everton and rescue a point in the 98th minute shows there is life in the old dog yet as did the victory at the Emirates. To me however, Sunday also made me angry because it proved to me that the players stopped playing for Jose. They wanted him out, the players are the same, but the attitude isn't.

2. Our football is without doubt more attacking. Some of our forward play against Everton and Arsenal was very encouraging and great to watch. Most particularly as up until the weekend we appeared to have completely lost the ability to defend. It is difficult to know whether this is due to a slight change in tactics, or players being less fearful of screwing up. Either way this has to be a good thing. We

still suffer from a lack of forward options, but we are certainly scoring more than we were.

3. Certain players appear to have played themselves back into form. The first game after Jose left, Oscar was simply brilliant... albeit it was against Sunderland... but he looked like a man released from some spell. I know that many are still not convinced by Oscar, but I like him and hope he stays at the club. There has also been a change in the form of Fabregas and Costa. Both have shown more hunger, and Costa has stopped hiding on the wing. If you compared his runs in his last couple of games to his static no show in Jose's last game the difference is staggering. A return to what he was producing last season is being helped by Cesc finding his magic hat. Is this all down to the change in management? We will never know.

4. Since Jose left we appear to be getting some decisions in our favour. I think we got back to back penalties and obviously against Everton we got a blatantly offside goal. I am not one for conspiracies, but surely referees are only human. If you or one of your colleagues have been constantly criticised by someone (and in a lot of cases rightly so) you are less likely to be favourable to that person whether directly or subconsciously. It's human nature. That being said, there have been few worse performances than Anthony Taylor against West Brom... and the lack of a penalty for Cesc was criminal.

5. We are off the back pages, and other managers are now getting the treatment from Fleet Street's finest albeit

no one to the extent of the hatchet job committed on Jose. That doesn't mean that we are not still subject to appalling stories. According to one tabloid, because Roman looked bored and fed up against Everton (and during the first half name one person who wasn't) he is going to sell the club. Another red top had a similar headline but the article under the headline actually said nothing of the sort, but hey why let the facts get in the way of a good story?

6. There are still two competitions to play for. We have a decent draw in the FA Cup, and there are no other teams tearing it up this season. In football clichés a good cup run could set us up for the rest of the season. Our team selection for the 3rd round angered the hell out of me but showed that we are going for it. As for the Champions League, whilst a big ask, our home performance against Porto suggested that this is a tournament the players will get out of bed for and if we can get a decent result in Paris anything is possible at the Bridge.

7. The youth have got some game time. Not enough in my book, but whole halves of football for RLC and Kenedy. Both did OK but need more game time. Also we shouldn't forget Zouma. He's having a storming season and is a great addition to the first team. To be fair, at the end of both the West Brom and Everton games he looked shell-shocked... but it's all good experience going forward and hopefully he will have a more solid defence around him next season.

8. OK, it almost barrel scraping time. Next is we

haven't done anything stupid in the transfer window. It does appear that we may be on the verge of doing something and some may argue that Charlie Austin going to Southampton for £4m is already negligent in the extreme. In terms of Pato he will not be match fit and I don't not look at our squad and say "blimey" we need another injury-prone forward to bolster our ranks. There is no doubt however potentially it could be something special. The continual refusal to give Patrick Bamford any game time is baffling. The chances of sensible long-term replacements coming into the squad in this window are unlikely, but let's not do anything stupid in the interim.

9. I'm finding it enjoyable to be watching football on the TV without every game meaning something. I can sit back and not care who beats who, sort of. Don't get me wrong there are a few teams I always want to lose but not caring is good. The sad thing is the Premiership is not of the highest standard. The recent 3-3 draw between Newcastle and Manchester United a case in point. Thoroughly entertaining, but mostly because of the comedy defending.

10. We are still Champions. I know that may sound desperate, but until some other team claims the crown, it's ours. It's an achievement which all too easily gets ignored or just downplayed. Commentators particularly love saying it in a sneering way as we are getting beaten Not only that, we were top from virtually day one. We should all remember there is no divine right to win, and the fact that

we have won 4 Premier League titles in 11 seasons is fantastic. So when people are having a go at all and sundry just remember that fact.

So there we go. Am I happy, of course not. Happy Birthday Jose, I miss you.

HOME COMFORTS

February 2016

I've not been 100% recently. Thankfully nothing serious, just a virus which won't shift. I missed the Manchester United game and at about 1.00 at home in the warm on Saturday I didn't feel much like dragging my weary body on the tube to the game. A relegation scrap against the barcodes that was on TV was not exactly a massive draw but the thought of more banal commentary and the wisdom of Redknapp was part of the incentive I needed to get out of the house. The other was my mates.

Missing football means also not meeting up with your buddies. It is after all part of the pre-game ritual. I've been going with the same guys for years. Usually it's a pre match beer or a pizza but feeling lousy nothing was appealing in that score so off to the stall to collect my cfcuk fanzine and say hi to DJ and Marco. You can always be sure of a cheery welcome especially if the weather has been particularly unkind. You are also assured of seeing more than few friendly faces and so it proved on Saturday.

As I got in the ground early I went and had a chat with one of my neighbours fellow blogger and top man Joe Tweeds. We spent a fine 20 odd minutes moaning about the season and trying to predict the future of the most unpredictable club in the land. I returned to my seat and waited for my guys to arrive which they did all at separate times, and all with their own lines of abuse for my absence from ground and pub/restaurant.

The team was semi-predictable with Pedro for Oscar and Obi on the bench, presumably protected for Paris. Feeling massively underwhelmed by the prospect of what was to come some 18 minutes later, my head was spinning. A tremendous onslaught had seen us score 3 goals against a particularly poor opposition. That however is unfair. Our first goal well crafted, the second superbly taken… and our third the best we've scored this season. Some of the stuff we were playing was scintillating. A million miles from the ponderous turgid fare that has been served up at the Bridge this season. We could and perhaps should have had a couple more in the first half but instead we had the sight of JT leaving the pitch and the feel good factor draining somewhat with the dark shadow of PSG rearing its ugly head.

Thankfully, apart from a 10 minute spell at the start of the second half, our defence was in the main not required and an absolutely sublime pass from Cesc to Pedro finished the game. Quite bucking the trend of completely baffling decisions of late, an infinitely sensible substitution of Diego for Bertrand followed as did an exquisitely taken striker's goal. With Baba on and Azpi being allowed to play on the right side, the vision of two full backs bombing on was evident since, well actually I can't remember.

I think Baba has been the unfortunate victim of politics

and the manager's devotion to a great club man in Brana. The guy has had hardly any game time and consequently looks less than solid when he plays but as was clear at the beginning of the MK Dons game he is keen to impress. With a run in the game, I think we potentially have a real player there. Once again it was good to see RLC get minutes, but with the state of the game he should in my opinion had a lot more. The hero of the season, Willian, could have been replaced earlier, but he looks like the sort of guy who never wants to come off.

Also a special mention for Matic whose performance was a welcome return to form. People will say he wasn't up against much, but ultimately you can only worry about your own form

The gaping hole in our midfield, and the goal conceded, was perhaps the consequence of a dead game drifting into oblivion but it would have been nice to have got another clean sheet. They have been rare this season and I am sure Thibaut would not have been pleased.

So I left the ground pleasantly surprised. There was a real hunger and desire in our performance even when we were coasting. I was really pleased. I had made the effort as the players had too.

With PSG in mind, my thoughts turn to Ray Mears. He would have most likely been asked to occupy a position on the left or right and just patrol a flank, but alas he has gone. He was one of the most baffling footballers I have ever had the pleasure of watching. A man who looked like he'd be hard pressed to stay on his feet on a windy day yet was hard as nails. A man who beautifully fits the phrase "he could trap a ball further than I could kick it" yet scored some of the most sublime and important goals.

A complete paradox. A Brazilian who couldn't pass, yet he could play in the most disciplined manner when requested to do so. Part of the legendary team who won in the Camp Nou in 2012. Part of a makeshift back four who played his heart out even though he knew he wasn't going to play in the final. The goal he scored that night will live forever in the hearts of Chelsea fans. His goals were normally exquisite, but ask him to pick out a blue shirt from 5 yards, not so easy. The amount of money that we have received is healthy and if it means that RLC steps into the squad to replace him I cannot be unhappy with the outcome. That being said, Ray is relatively young to be hanging up his boots… and I suspect he will be back in Europe in the not too distant future.

So long and thank you Ray.

WELCOME BACK

There was a moment during the Manchester City cup game when I turned round to my mate and said, "I love Jose but WTF did he do to these players?" It's fair to say the opposition was not the finest, but the change in the players, and the fact they are all playing to their full potential, sadly speaks volumes for the character traits of both the players and the Special One. A sad indictment of all involved.

A come-from-behind win against Southampton felt like the old spirit and passion was returning. Winning ugly. There is nothing wrong with that, we have been doing it for years. I try to be honest in my appraisal of how we play, but I have been shocked at the reports I've read that implied we were lucky to win. For me if a team sits back on a one nil lead for the whole of the second half without any attempt to increase that lead... they get what they deserve.

I thought the hooking of Baba was incredibly harsh and hope he is back for Norwich. I like the new dynamism through our full backs. The substitution worked and ultimately that is all that counts. If however you were looking to hook people off for making a mistake, half that team could've come off. I spend a lot of time defending Thibaut, but he was asleep for the goal. If he had started to come when the mistake was made he would have been on top of the striker before he got near the goal. There is something not quite right about our keeper at the moment and I'm not too sure what it is.

One thing that I particularly enjoyed on Saturday was the knowledge that there was more to be had once we equalised. A draw would have been respectable, but once we scored we continued to go forward. There was no thought of keeping what we had. The team are hungry again and that is good to see. I would be fascinated to know what the team think is achievable this season and whether looking at Leicester sitting at the top of the league they regret not turning up for the first 3 months of the season.

Three 5-1 victories in our last 7 games is very reminiscent of the football we were playing last time Guus was here, albeit with less impressive squad. Hunting in packs and attacking with speed. It's interesting the transformation and the hunger the players now seem to have. I wrote previously about Oscar. A player who massively divides the fans. I am a big fan but understand why his detractors are not so sure. A 20 minute jog against City which was whatever the word is for the reverse of a cameo. Maybe a camembert because it stunk. Yet his improvement since Jose left is there for all to see. He was a player who was hooked whenever he made a mistake under Jose and now he is playing with freedom.

That being said, I wasn't pleased to see him against City. Why oh why was he brought on and RLC left on the bench? 4-1 up against a weak team, when do the young players get game time? Where was Kenedy? Why also not bring on Miazga for the last 15 minutes, Cahill certainly looked in the wars. A moan after a win but I think a justifiable questioning of the manager's mindset.

At the beginning of the season, I was asked to do a prediction column for the Standard which I was thrilled to do... but what a mug. I, like most, got virtually everything wrong, but my biggest boast was that signing Jose to a new deal was the best bit of business we could do. Whilst wiping that particular piece of egg from my face I did however say that the one player I thought may break through this season was Bertrand Traore. He looks a great player, fast and a great eye for a goal and certainly not a left back! I had to laugh when he scored against City thinking what Torres would have given for such fortune (or did he mean it). I like Berty and the fact he is now getting a chance. With hopefully 6 more points in the bag in the league soon and some other kids may get an outing, or maybe not!

I know this is a Chelsea book, but if I was a City fan reading it I'd still be angry. It cannot be right that you can just decide that you do not want to compete in a tournament so you give up. I can excuse a small club with a thin squad who are desperate to stay in the Premier League, but the richest club in the world? What difference would it had made if they played at least three more experienced players to their chances against Kiev? None. I appreciate that Audrey told the fans what was coming, but there is no excuse for what happened. I am sure it wasn't Audrey's decision entirely but I do not want that man anywhere near our managerial swivel chair.

The one downside of our upturn in form is that I am now watching MOTD again. Despite his penalty heroics in the League Cup Final, City's stand in keeper is poor. His bizarre movement for Hazard's goal was not impressive... but for Danny Murphy to describe the goal as a goalkeeping error and give no merit to the free kick was twaddle. Some are still on Hazard's back. I have said I do not think he is 100% match fit and I think his body language does him no favours, but his recent performances are encouraging.

LAST CHANCE SALOON

March 2016

I do not think it's an exaggeration to say that this close season is the most important for the club since probably 1983. After the end of our season, at around 7.20 at Goodison Park on March 12, following our defeat in the 6th round of the FA Cup, there has been a huge amount of accusation and finger pointing... but the facts as I see them are as follows.

In the last 12-18 months we have let our squad disintegrate from one of the strongest to one of the most average in the Premier League. This can be blamed on bad sales, awful purchases, and a reluctance to trust youth. There was also a quaint belief that we were adhering to FFP which it appeared no one else was. It is ultimately irrelevant as to whose fault it is or was. We are there now and the question has to be how should it be addressed?

We had one of the strongest set of players and team ethic the Premier league had ever seen. It was a once in a lifetime squad and it was inevitable that it would not last forever. Certain players were irreplaceable, but what they have been replaced by is distinctly average overpriced imitations.

So a new manager will be brought in but quite frankly it could be the Chuckle Brothers unless they are allowed to get on with it without external interference. Yes they need money, but with one of the richest owners in world football and a quite frankly obscene amount of money from TV… the rebuilding should not be hampered by a lack of funds. So what is done next is important because getting back to the top table of English and then European football is on a knife edge.

Despite Guus steadying the ship, it is fair to say that the last week has summed up what a decidedly unmotivated and average squad we have. So where are we in terms of personnel and what do we need?

Goalkeepers.

Despite the constant and at times totally unwarranted criticism this is the one area we do not need to change anything in my opinion. TC has not had a great season but at 23, do people really want to get rid of him?

Full Backs.

We have all been clamouring for Azpi to play in his rightful position, and in the main we have got what we want. With more protection in front of him… and better players next to him he can excel. I understand that Aina is a decent prospect, but because of lack of opportunities he is set to leave so we need a back up. We also need at least one left back. Unfortunately Baba appears too flakey and does not appear to be likely to be given a chance. Personally, I would just leave him in the team until the end of the season and see where we are after that. We also have a great youth product in Jay Dasilva. It is said that his size may count against him but he is unlikely to be the answer for next season.

Centre Backs.

Here is a major problem. All of our current centre backs are OK and sadly nothing more. Yesterday, Gary Cahill was again shown up. Brana is a decent player, and JT appears to be history. We can only speculate as to what state Kurt will be in when he returns, but if he is still in decent shape he showed he is a good prospect but he will need a mature player beside him. We shouldn't forget we also have Andreas Christensen doing well in the Bundesliga. He is on a two year loan and I suspect we could call him back and I personally think we should. If we do get Conte expect at least two no-nonsense centre backs to come in

Midfield.

This for me this has been our biggest problem, sadly highlighted in the Champions League. Against PSG they had no Verratti (the sort of player we desperately need) so in came Rabiot to join Matuidi and Moura. Perhaps an extreme comparison, but at one time we could call on Makelele, Essien, Ballack, Lampard and Cole.

With the exception of Willian, I would not be sad to lose any of our current squad with the caveat that I need to see RLC play in whatever his proper position is before he is "written off". For me this is the biggest cause of concern. We have no engine and no drive, and we are one paced and predictable. Ordinary teams have consistently out run us this season without too much difficulty. We create very little by way of chances. Players like Oscar have clearly not trained hard enough. I admire Pedro's work rate but he is currently not a player for the Premier League and certainly not what we needed when purchased.

Forwards.

I would like to keep Costa and we have Traore. I think that Remy has been badly treated but he has recently looked like he cannot be bothered. Next year there is the possibility of Musonda being given a chance and there is also both Solanke and Abraham. There is no doubt that we need at least one or two additions if we are to compete.

Hazard.

A section all to himself! I personally believe he has not been fit for the vast majority of this season. At the beginning he was just unforgivably both overweight and unfit. We then had Evagate and if that affected him that is just one of those things... but his form continued to be poor. He got injured at Leicester... whatever anyone says, and has not been fully fit since. He pulled up when taking a shot against Palace. I noticed when he took a shot against Stoke he pulled up once more and again against PSG. Personally I'd leave him out now until the end of the season. If he wants to go, so be it... but FFS don't boo him. I was disgusted at a large section of our fans that booed him off the pitch against PSG. I didn't know about the shirt swapping when I was at the game but had he scored the winner that night would anyone have cared?

Just remember when we've got some third rate trier giving his all to beat his man and failing miserably that some rushed Hazard out of the club. The question is whether anyone else would want him in their team? And we all know the answer.

So whoever is entrusted to rebuild our club let's hope they are allowed to do a good job as it's a long way back otherwise.

YOUTH, YOUTH AND YOUTH

However you dress it up, this season has not been good. Half way through the West Ham home game I thought why did we sack Jose? The club is out of the papers, but we are out of everything else as well. The team was back to its unbalanced defence, turgid midfield and passenger performances.

Then something happened. Youth appeared and we had some pace and desire. It was no coincidence that the team caught fire when first Traore and then RLC appeared. Whatever delusion Guus has, we are not getting a European place and so there is no risk in playing more kids.

Much as I think Remy has been appallingly treated in terms of team selection, it's fair to say every time he has played recently he has stunk the place out. We all know, including him, that he's off at the end of the season… so from now to the end of the season play Traore, even when Diego is fit. Also watching Rashford in the Manchester derby it is interesting to reflect that he was in the United youth team beaten 5-1 by our boys earlier this season. Our scorers that night were Ugbo, Abraham, Mount, Dasilva and Ali. What chance any of them getting a game before the end of this dead season?

As much as I like Obi, he has done his job and I would start RLC. It's fair to say he did not impress against Stoke, but yesterday it looked like he was given freedom and when he ran at people he looked menacing. I don't think anyone knows where his best position is but running from deep he looked good.

Until his injury, Kenedy looked good. Indeed he was the only thing that did. Personally I would start Baba behind him and those two would cover for each other. Let's face it our defence has been a shambles and so this combination couldn't do any worse.

In the pub after the game there were lots of calls for Thibaut to be dropped. I agree he has not been great but how horribly exposed has he been? Yet again Brana was skinned or nowhere to be seen at right back. Personally, I can see no benefit in dropping Thibaut apart from rewarding Begovic's patience.

So yet another draw on Saturday, but it could have been so much less. Great spirit to come back led by Cesc. Many are calling for him to be skipper next year. I'm not sure, but really cannot point to anyone else. When he scored for me it showed how much it mattered. If it is Conte, he can be our Pirlo, we shall see.

The one thing which showed clearly on Saturday was how when you are not used to being in an elevated position there is no substitute for experience. There was no one in that West Ham side who could direct that team to the 3 points. They should have had the game won long before we got back into it. I looked at Payet and wondered what exactly is missing from Oscar an undoubted talent who gave another lacklustre performance. I am willing him to do well, and in a no pressure game on Saturday he was flat and disappointing. Another unsolved mystery.

So please Guus forget about your unbeaten record. Let's see some passion youth and pace. "Play the youth" has been a statement mocked on social media by many. No one is saying we want 11 youth players, but each side until the end of the season should have at least four. I said a couple of months ago, if we have a transitional season it would be bearable if we got some kids in the squad. We are heading that way, if he recovers, Kurt, Kenedy and Traore are three. Let's get at least one more. So if any of them mis-control the ball get caught offside shoot wide. Give them some slack, they are learning and we will benefit.

THIBAUT OR NOT THIBAUT?

April 2016

It has been another question in a number of things which is dividing fans opinions this season. Where has TC gone, it's not quite "Where's Wally?" but it's an equally difficult puzzle. During the early part of last season, I remember Gary Neville picking out TC for praise as he was coming out for the ball and holding not punching. He cut a huge imposing figure immediately relieving any pressure on his defenders. He commanded his area. He came for highballs not just from crosses.

That however is a very different goalkeeper to the one we have at the moment. He seems tentative in most things he does, most particularly when coming off his line and in one on one situations. In fact he looks like he is lacking in confidence. There are however a few things which I would like to put in his defence.

The first thing is his age. He is only 23 yet he already has won the league in two separate countries. He, like Hazard, up until this season has only had success and probably for the first time in their respective careers they are suffering a blip.

A lot of what he does gets taken for granted. There are times I feel when he makes things look easy when perhaps they are not. During the PSG game in Paris it was commented he had a lot to do but all the saves he made were ones you would expect him to make. Is that because they were easy or he made them easier by his positioning? I think the latter.

This will without doubt have been the worst defence he would have played behind. Despite the plaudits Brana and Cahill have got recently, whether due to tiredness or lack of midfield cover it has to be said the ease with which the mighty Norwich cut them apart was scary. The back four is a problem that Jose couldn't seem to sort out and that says it all.

I also think (without any direct proof) that Cech would have been some form of mentor to TC. Such is the nature and stature of the man, ignoring his own hurt at no longer being number 1 he would have gone out of his way to help TC. With him not there this must be a void. There is also talk that he is less than enamoured with Lollichon which would not help and needs to be sorted

Like other players in the team this season his drop off in form has been dramatic but there are more factors in addition to the above at play in my opinion. He was sent off in the first game of this season. A lacklustre attempt at a tackle which was poor and may have led to him being much slower of his line and less committed to coming off his line so quickly during the rest of the season. We don't know how that was dealt with on the coaching side but he certainly looks tentative to say the least. He was nowhere near preventing the Southampton goal at Saint Mary's which we all know was down to an error by Baba, but if he had been quicker off his line it would have made things more difficult for the striker. There seems to be a reluctance to confront strikers or dive at their feet.

Of course none of us know how he was affected by the knee injury he suffered. Was it more serious than disclosed and has this hampered his movement in any way? From a distance for me he seems less focused. He seems very slow to read the game and less engaged with the rest of his defence. The fact he never digs out his defender or seems to show any real emotion however inaccurate probably dictates a lot of the public perception.

We also have no idea what affect the Charlie Adams lob has affected his positioning and a reluctance to leave his line.

So all of these are excuses, but what are we left with. At the moment a good but not great goalkeeper who is getting stick from the fans when it is not always appropriate. For example against Stoke he had pulled off two very good saves to help us protect our lead. He however is blamed by some for their equaliser despite not being the person who lost the ball on the half way line nor was he any of the outfield players who failed to put a tackle in before the ball got anywhere near him. Yet his effort to try and reach the ball is all that is seen and talked about. Could he have done better? Maybe, but it seems that every little thing is being punished at the moment.

Again at home to West Ham he is taking the blame for

the Andy Carroll goal but again he is left horribly exposed. How many goals have we conceded from that flank?

He seems to favour his right hand side. The Lukaku "wonder" goal in the FA Cup defeat was a horror show of missed tackles, but TC showed him right and the left was open.

It may seem harsh to heap so much criticism on him, but he had set such high standards it is difficult not to be disappointed at what we have seen this year. It appears however that TC's main crime for which he can never be acquitted is that he is not Petr Cech. This is perhaps the least fair and most erroneous of arguments. The Cech that left us was not the Cech that joined us.

In addition before Cech was marshalled by Terry, Carvalho, Gallas, Cole, Ferreira pre-supposing anyone could get through the small matter of Makelele and Essien. We all know why Cech was sold, but surely we wouldn't have been much better off with Cech in goal instead of TC this season. When Petr joined he won back to back titles. Well TC won a title in his first year and it's not his fault he has had to be custodian behind the worst defence we have had in years. I think the crowd like to see passion from the players, but as stated TC is very phlegmatic… but so was Cech whose name was never chanted until he was out of the team.

This season is turning into hunt the scapegoat. Personally, I think any sale of TC will be a huge mistake and only justifiable with a top class replacement. If Conte is coming, I would hope that TC would give it another season. Time will tell.

BENVENUTO

We have a new manager with a tailor made name for puns. So am I excited beyond belief as I have loved all but one of the Italian managers we've had so far? Well not really, but that has got nothing to do with Conte, I'm just very sceptical.

What I do know is that he has been a successful player and now manager. I've read lots about how he loves to do this that and the other, but what he does here will be dependent on various factors. I also know that sadly every misplaced pass by an Italian player in the Euros will be looked upon by the great and the good of social media as being incontrovertible truth that we have employed a dud. You know it's true.

So what can we expect? I would imagine Conte will be given some money and he will be able to bring in some players who will fit in to the style of football he will want to play. He may possibly be encouraged to use some of our academy players in his squad and I would imagine that he has been watching a lot of them since his official appointment.

He may possibly bring back Juan Cuadrado who apparently has turned into the best player on the planet since he left us. He was certainly one of the worst before he went. I suspect the truth is somewhere in the middle but we shall see.

He may announce that he couldn't possibly do the job without JT being part of his team. This maybe something that is part of an initial charm offensive but I have a sneaking suspicion he will bring in his own Italian enforcers. Personally, I think he would be foolish to get rid of JT but that as we all know is another story.

As an Italian of the "old school" I am expecting and indeed hoping Conte repairs our defence. It is sadly broken and has been a huge problem this year. It was interesting to see that even Villa and more latterly Bournemouth found their way through without much difficulty. It was only their complete lack of interest that prevented them scoring. It's difficult to pin point why it is so bad, but bad it is. As we know a side defends all over the pitch and midfield is where we need a general. Someone who kicks first and asks questions afterwards. It seems that Conte's teams have always had that sort of player and he hopefully has a black book full of numbers.

I do not intend to dissect the squad and say who should stay or go, but whoever stays needs to want to be there. This I hope more than anything else is something he will be able to instil back in the club. Yes we look better than we have in the first part of the season but that isn't hard.

So to the elephant in the room, whether our new manager will be able to manage? Not his ability but whether he will be allowed to manage his way through the level of interference which has been in place? We as a club need to get away from a style of club management which we currently have. If he is not allowed to get on with what he wants to, then what is the point of employing a decent manager? From what I have read and heard about him he seems strong willed and it may be that the club have decided that is what they need. So maybe we can have a period of stabilisation before he has the rug pulled from under him (no pun intended).

It seems churlish to moan about my club when we have won so much more than I could possibly have dreamt of, but the scatter gun purchase of players without any real thought has come home to roost. The punch bag for fans is Emenalo, but not one of us has an idea what he actually does or what he has actually been responsible for. The nadir of our transfer policy was the purchase of Papa and Hector. Both players bought without the manager wanting or knowing about them. On top of that, this was a slap in the face to him and every decent youth player at the club or on loan.

We then had the Pato deal. With the appointment of Conte, I now wonder whether he was parked here to get fit and see how he settled in. Well the signs were good when he made his goal-scoring debut, albeit in the context of the opposition, against possibly the worst team in Premier league history. He however looked rather pleased to be here, which is more than can be said for a few this season.

In terms of his coaching staff, let him choose his own.

I hope there is a place for Steve Holland who seems a decent man. If there is, it will show me that Conte appreciates he will need help in learning about the players and the league. He will have spoken to others who will have all expressed an opinion, but he looks like a man who knows his own views and will not suffer fools gladly.

The main worry is when will be able to get things put in place? The final of the Euros is on 10 July 2016 and the start of the Premier League season is 13 August 2016. Most teams in the Premier League will have players away but not their manager. So who does what? Will Guus be there to start the training and then we are off on our world tour again with no lessons learnt. I do not want to deny any of our wonderful Stateside supporters the opportunity to see our guys, but the timings here are really not ideal for what is our most important season in decades. I suspect these things have been thought about and discussed, but with Conte's Italy duties who has been delegated to start things off? Perhaps an ex Nigerian footballer?

I do know that one of the reasons Conte fell out with Juve was his displeasure with an overseas pre-season tour. Just saying...

OSCAR WILD?

It's not often that you read about Oscar Wilde (see what I did there?) being quoted in a football context, but he said there is only one thing worse than being talked about, and that is not being talked about. What a perfect summary of where we were this season.

In some respects, it is great to be off the back pages. So we were last yet again on MOTD and barely getting a mention anywhere in the media. Only the re-emergence of Eden causing a slight ripple of interest and that to be honest was only in respect of his comments about the game against Spurs. When the season finishes and the transfer rumours are again swirling, we will re appear. We all know the cr@p will begin in earnest when Conte is in place. So perhaps we should enjoy the anonymity after all the end of this season is a combination between boredom and frustration

So we had a fine away win against Bournemouth which ironically and quite usefully was played near the beach which both teams at the time were actively occupying. I was fairly hacked off when I saw the team. It was yet another game that barely mattered and yet no youth players were in sight. The sight of Obi Wan in defence and poor young Matt on the bench! We were playing against a poor team yet the American was unable to make an appearance. These are for all intents and purposes practice matches. It seems obvious therefore that Matt has no future at the club. His non appearance makes the loan circuit inevitable.

The lack of RLC was more understandable and it was good to see Matic back. At 3-1 up with 20 minutes plus to go why no Kenedy or Traore though? What are we saving them for? Berty had built up a nice head of steam and now he barely gets a look in. It's completely unacceptable in my book. I wasn't there and didn't see the pattern of play but IT DIDN'T MATTER WHAT HAPPENED so what was the rationale Guus?

I have defended Eden this season. The low point of the boos and the derision when he left the field of play at Palace and Leicester. I have always said he was not fit. Initially match fitness was not really acceptable, but the injuries were real. Call me deluded, but his joy was obvious to see and he was just glad to fully fit and playing football again. I sincerely hope he doesn't leave.

Pedro is a funny player. Not in the belly laugh sense, but I cannot place him in terms of team structure. He is a great finisher. I like his effort and commitment, but is he not what we need. He may go in the summer or perhaps stay as a squad player. It will be interesting to see if Conte wants to use him going forward.

The same could be said of Cesc. Will he become Conte's Pirlo? When he is left alone, not harassed nor called into defensive duties, he is a maestro. Pulling the strings and frankly ripping Bournemouth to shreds he produced an absolute masterclass. If he can be protected by a couple of enforcers, I have a feeling we will be a team full of speed next season and someone providing those defence splitting passes will be essential.

So where is Oscar? Not feeling well last week, and nowhere to be seen yesterday. What is happening? Has he received assurances he is a big part of next season so he has the time off or the opposite? He will be at the Copa America in the summer and yet only Willian's plans are being talked about. Many have scratched their heads because of the money we allegedly turned down for him, but I perhaps naively am hoping that he does finally emerge. Some have speculated that because Conte is a harsh task master Oscar won't fancy it. Time will tell.

Watching the FA Cup semi final was a tough ask. To see Everton's inept first half display (their injuries notwithstanding) I felt a sense deep frustration at our meek surrender at Goodison Park. Even though I detest Wembley as a semi final venue I wanted it to be us there. Neither team looked anything to fear but I appreciate that is rich in our current position and so I was left to ponder, what if.

I was extremely amused at the Twitter meltdown against young Romelu. Poor chap. Playing in a team where attack and midfield were disconnected, he ran his heart out. He missed a couple of presentable chances and of course there was the penalty. It will come as no surprise that I call it a penalty save and not a penalty miss. A simply superb save, but these chances have to be taken.

Do I want him back at the club? Well it depends on so many different factors. I would rather have Costa if we intend to labour on as a sole striker but are we about to change our formations? He is still quite young but personally I would like us to end the lone striker formation and ultimately that would mean he may not be what we are looking for. All that being said, whilst he didn't have a good game in the semi-final his goal scoring ratio is very good. We got good money and maybe he genuinely wants to come back. But I'm not convinced.

I do however hope we go back for Stones. A fine prospect, English and just imagine how he would be if he was properly coached by an Italian with perhaps some chiselled old pro next to him. You do have to wonder what St Martinez has done to him this season or maybe the young man believed the hype. Yes he's made mistakes, but as I have said about our own young players, that is what they do. They have to learn, and its inevitable errors will occur.

So Spurs were upset by Eden Hazard saying what everyone in football feels, we all want Leicester rather than THem to win the league. Small question, would THem beating Leicester at home not have saved their angst?

HOLLOW

May 2016

Following the draw with Spurs, I felt the elation of stopping a rival. The petty snarling slagging off our celebrations is sour grapes. What would they have done had they stopped Arsenal in the same way? So why am I so angry?

The date of the game was 1 May 2016 and the league season started on 8 August 2015. Where the hell have most of our players been during the intervening period? (I exclude both Willian and Cesar) I am angry because had we played like we did in the second 45 minutes of that game for the majority of the season, we would have won a hell of a lot more games than we have, or at least competed!

Where was that passion and will to win or at least not to lose when Jose was clinging on to his job for dear life? I tell you where, nowhere. Those players have given very little this season and quite frankly it's inexcusable. I am not saying we would have won anything but we would be a lot closer than we are now.

Where was that aggression and spirit when we limped out of the FA cup at Goodison Park? That was one of the most passionless gutless displays since our exit to Swansea in the League Cup a couple of years ago. Had they shown some of that fight then we might be looking forward to Wembley instead of three meaningless games.

We have known all along that these players had that ability. So why this game? Was it just to appease the fans who they know they have let down this season? Why hasn't Guus been able to get this sort of performance from them until now?

The only line of defence is that in the second half of the game we had a fit Eden Hazard. I have defended the guy both in blogs and on the podcasts. I have said that he has not been fit for the vast majority of the season. Against Spurs he was being kicked again, proof if it were needed that he is back to his best. Too late in the season for us, but ready for the Euros and hopefully next season.

Protecting the 26 years was achieved, the taunting delivered and the Twitter meltdown and ludicrous statements flew. At the end of it all, the players showed pride. I have seen it said that it is unlikely Guus gave the half time team talk and I think that must be right. It was probably the man being shown the door who probably rammed home a few home truths at half time. JT, the man who brilliantly put on his Instagram account after the game **#notonmywatch**. I also suspect that Cesc with his Arsenal hat on rather than his magic one was equally vociferous. All great but we seemed to have won (or drawn) the battle but lost the war.

Now I have got that off my chest what about the game itself? It was a throwback the challenges flew in and for those of us of a certain age it was back to the "good" old days when men were men and didn't roll around because someone stood on their hand. That being said, some of THeir tackles were bad. The referee was awful as usual but now the game has finished part of me is glad that there were no sending's off. Less excuses for them to fall back on. My view may well have been different had we needed to win the game and the opposition quite inexplicably kept 11 men on the pitch.

I had been listening and reading with interest about what some of our fans thought we were going to do against Spurs and how we were going to let Leicester win if that was what was required. Really? Have you seen us play this season? Nothing other than their own nerves would have stopped Leicester getting whatever they needed at the Bridge. They are simply a better team than us this season, team being the operative word. This is now a non point as they come to us as Champions and as we know anyone who achieves that deserves it.

Our second half display should not paper over the cracks. We were listless with no creativity in the first half, picked off at will by a better team. A flat defence breached for the first goal, and a gift for the second. The game had been fairly even up to the first goal but with two defensive midfielders starting and not much coming from either Cesc or Pedro thing were looking bleak at half time.

I could understand Guus's thinking in trying to keep it tight initially but on the basis Eden had played a full 90 minutes 9 days ago, I was confused as to why our best player was on the bench. Apart from one snapshot, Diego appeared to have retreated into early season mode where he was loitering on the wing but he was feeding off scraps with no support.

I thought that Willian was disappointing but still full of effort. The funny thing was the chant implying that that he was not very good followed by him pointing at his Champions badge seemed to give him the kick start he needed. After half time he, like the others, was back to his best. Although we still looked vulnerable at the back, their tough-tackling seemed to galvanise us… and once Cahill scored Spurs looked nervous.

To describe Eden's goal as good is doing him a disservice. It was similar to the goal he scored against Spurs last season, cutting in from the same wing… but the interplay with Diego sublime. Quite naturally the Bridge went wild, and from that point onwards if anyone was to win it would have been us.

I'd like to specifically pick out Cesar for praise. I thought he was immense. He at no stage looked like he had given up and we are lucky to have him. Maybe under Conte he will continue at left back.

I feel that if the highlight of our season is stopping a rival winning the league that says it all. I will not keep on about Jose, but I would interested to know the clubs ambitions when he was sacked. Presumably more than 2 home league wins (only 1 under Guus). Perhaps further in the cups and higher in a bang average league? I do not believe that Guus's brief was avoiding relegation. Qualification for Europe must have been the expectation. We all know that Jose was not blameless but I still do not think that we are in a better place now without him.

So this mess of a season draws to an end. We still have 9 points to play for and the final day of the season homage to Emperor Claudio. I have no great love for the guy. He didn't have the easiest of tasks but got us into the Champions League, the pre cursor to the Abramovich era. Yes he showed an enormous amount of class when he left. He gave us that night at Highbury which will live long in the memory, but he also gave us Monaco. I am not sure all of the players loved him... but Frank has paid tribute to him, and so I will pay my respects.

Finally, however much as the game meant, in my opinion we should never chant the name of another team in our stadium. As for that cardboard banner saying we should do it for Claudio....no, we should do it for us first and last, end of!

FOXED THAT UP

I think that if you met my mate and neighbour Roger you'd like him. He's a Bon Viveur, great company and loves his sport… especially football. He supports Leicester and if you'd said at the start of the season that one of our teams would win the league this year we both would have said it will be my team.

When we won on that famous night in Munich, I have always said that I wanted every genuine football fan to experience what I felt that night. The sheer joy coupled with the incredulity of what I had just witnessed. It's for that reason I wanted Leicester to win the league for Roger. There is no way he would have thought that this day was ever coming. I suspect like us at Bolton, the tears will flow and it will be a momentous day.

What I did not want is them winning it at our place. For those old enough to remember, it was horrible the day Kenny Dalglish won it with Liverpool at the Bridge. Even though we were utter pants then and there was no rivalry, I hated that day. The guard of honour is bad enough, but spare us the clincher being at home. I remember drink had been taken and I was screaming and shouting at our players to not just accept the inevitable. I was politely told at half time by a member of the Metropolitan Police to keep it down and needless to say neither I nor the team had the appetite or indeed ability to stop the reds that day.

Let's be honest though we all wanted Leicester to win as the thought of anyone "proper" winning it scared us. Having to live with a Spurs win is more than anyone could have taken.

For me, Leicester City means Alan Birchenall and Keith Weller... the old Filbert Street ground, but more than anything they will always mean Steve Guppy. For the first time in my memory we were close enough to challenge for the title. It was 18 April 1999 and I was in Majorca. I remember the bar I saw the game in was traditional and painted in green and white. I was sat watching one of those TVs mounted on the wall with my mate Andy. We were 2-0 up and coasting.

It's the 82nd minute and Doobs diverts a shot into his own net. Panic sets into our defence until then virtually untroubled, and Leicester start to dominate a game they were out of. With two minutes to go Steve Guppy cuts in from the left and scores past big Ed. That sight of Martin O'Neill leaping up and down like a pogo stick left me feeling sick to the stomach.

Our first title challenge for nearly 30 years was gone. We left the pub dazed. We sat on the beach watching the sea trying to take in what had just happened. We encountered a feeling of utter desolation. In fact, it's in my top ten of worst Chelsea moments... and believe me there are some real horrors in there. I will remember that moment if and when it comes to applauding them.

Personally I also don't get the love for Ranieri. It is not

my annoyance that my tweet following his appointment that he'd be gone by Easter has been relentlessly retweeted! Name me one person who thought this was going to happen. No, I didn't like him as soon as he arrived. He replaced Vialli, so from the start I didn't like him… so obviously my initial dislike was completely irrational. He did little to endear himself to me during his time at the club. I think he did a decent job at times in difficult circumstances, but people seem to forget the constant tinkering. The frustration of his bizarre substitutions none more so than that game in Monaco. How did we go from 1 nil up against 10 men to 3-1 down?

My memory of that night was seeing Frank Lampard turning to the bench after another ridiculous substitution to ask WTF was going on to be greeted by a shrug of the shoulders. I had a perfect view from where I was sitting and saw CR either didn't care or had completely lost the plot. I know that Jose was in Monaco for his job interview and CR knew he was on his way out, but what better way of sticking two fingers up at Roman than beating Jose on your way to winning the CL? He had managed in Spain and Italy. He knew the score but bottled it. There is no way with that team we should have got knocked out by Monaco.

I know that a lot of our fans hold him in high esteem and that is fair enough. I was happy to see him go and be replaced by Jose. Interesting that some people earlier this season suggested Roman must be regretting appointing

Jose and not CR as Leicester continued to do well. Really? Up until this year CR has won nothing. That would be my biggest fear, but let's hope he does it as we all know what the alternative is.

So another season draws to a close and it is hard to believe that a year ago we were getting ready for the return of the Premier League trophy to the club. A fantastic day of celebration. How different the atmosphere at the Bridge will be for this game. It may be nail biting, but for no other reason than wanting a certain team not to win the league.

A lot has been written about our sad demise this season, but let's look forward and sincerely hope that this season has been a blip. By way of perspective I was informed before the Villa game that this was the first time in 23 years at that stage of the season we were out of contention for anything. Take a moment ladies and gentlemen. Nearly a quarter of a century. This did not necessarily mean we won things all the time in that period, but it shows how successful our club has been.

So Forza Conte, and I hope you guys summer well and just because Italy don't do well this summer it doesn't mean that you are not getting a damn fine manager!

WHAT'S ALL THE GUUS ABOUT?

After the 2009 FA Cup final I remember my Everton supporting mate taking the mickey of the chants for Guus Hiddink to stay. I was gutted he wasn't staying on. He did a great job and couldn't understand why he wouldn't. The players obviously loved him but it was not meant to be.

As the end of his second spell approaches there will not be much chanting for him I suspect. It's hard to know what to think. I'm writing this before we lose away to Liverpool and draw with Leicester but I think if that were actually the case his win percentage would actually be worse than Jose's.

So what exactly was his mandate when he came in? Well the most commonly used cliché was to "steady the ship". That nasty Portuguese man had upset some of the players and we wouldn't want that, so we get rid of him and bring in the loveable Guus. The players rejoice and within weeks that listing ship has been righted and we are saved from certain relegation. Well that takes us up to January and then what?

Well not a lot. There was a sterile transfer window which saw the arrival of a completely unfit striker and a "prospect". Both of whom will have played in total less than 2 games each since their respective arrivals in January. In other words a pointless exercise when there are players at the club or on loan who are potentially both equal to or if not better than both of them. Hard to know if Guus was in any way involved.

Notwithstanding our league position when Jose was sacked, with the number of games left a European place was well within our grasp. Since Guus arrived we have won a single home league game but his record away from the Bridge is more than acceptable and had it been replicated at home we would comfortably be sitting 5th or 6th.

The cups were slightly better although the exit to PSG in the Champions League was predictable despite the away leg being one of our better performances this season. With more clinical finishing from Diego we may have got even more. The home leg was close before Diego got injured, but the game finished with a whimper. PSGs vastly superior squad showed how far we had fallen in that regard. There's not anything Guus could have done about that, but when we needed to throw the kitchen sink at the last 25 minutes… the white flag was waved and we didn't even use all of our substitutes.

The FA Cup was our only realistic chance of silverware. We played Scunthorpe at home, and showing almost a paralysis of fear Guus did not pick one kid against a team in the third tier of football. A turgid 2-0 victory followed. That being said, the next two games, the demolition of MK Dons and Manchester City, youth was given a chance and Traore was on the score sheet for both games. We had started scoring lots of goals, and the 2009

Guus appeared to have entered the building.

However following the exit to PSG we then went Everton in the quarter final of the cup… a thoroughly woeful performance. As they set about Diego (as many have), his colleagues stood by and the game was summed up perfectly by JT coming on for the 10 men with a couple of minutes to go to play as a centre forward with us already 2-0 down. This was a passionless display against average opponents. The team that day was made up of a lot of the players who played against THem at home. That should tell us everything about those players and the manager that we need to know.

The team at times have not been helped by selections. The Matic/Mikel partnership whilst solid makes us slower than a turning oil tanker. The away game against Watford was there for the taking, but we were too scared to go for it. There has been a complete lack of any ambition. We were never going down

There have been some decent performances, especially at the Emirates, but let's face it Swansea have won there as did Watford. Other performances have been poor in a weak Premier League we have looked what we are an average team that has been worked out. You can't blame Guus for being without the best player in the club for most of his tenure, but there does not ever appear to have been a plan B.

All that being said, you have always had the impression from day one that he is being told what to do. By who is another story but there appear to be a lot of people at the club who are "running" or should I say ruining it.

I think my biggest criticism of Guus is since the exit from the cup, every game has been meaningless. Yes we may have been able to qualify for the Europa League, but our performances all season have shown this was not going to happen. So in those circumstances, how many of our young players have started a game? I think that Baba, RLC, Traore and Kenedy have barely 10 appearances if that between them. Why, does Guus still think we are going down?

What has been his mandate? What possible consequence could there be for not playing some of these guys? They could hardly have done any worse. Invaluable experience could have been obtained, but that has all been lost. In contrast look at what Klopp has done. He's played loads of kids, and in circumstances where they have had a genuine chance of European qualification through their league position. It would be fascinating to know what he would have done with our promising crop of kids.

This season has been about treading water since Jose left. To me there has not been any effort at all to move the club forward. It feels like it was written off and that's it. I cannot point to one positive as this season comes to a conclusion. The success of our youth teams is pointless and not worth celebrating if we enter into another season without any of them being given a sniff of a first team place. Maybe they aren't good enough, but, as I have said before, Marcus Rashford was in the Manchester United team that lost 5-1 to Chelsea in the Youth Cup. I cannot accept that Tammy Abraham has had very few minutes.

Managing our club has become almost impossible and yet until this year the trophies accumulated. There has however been a concerted effort to dismantle the great team of Cech, Cole, Lampard, Terry and Drogba... and time moves on, so that had to be right... but where it has fallen down is the lack of integration of other similar players. Now they were greats, and that would have been difficult... but with the exception of Cole and Cech those other guys did not hit the ground running.

It looks like Guus will be with us next year. He will transition the youngsters in to the team apparently. Perhaps that's something he should have been doing this year?

WHAT DOES IT STILL MATA?

When you were growing up, was there anything worse than watching an ex-partner for whom you still had great affection with their new beau?

Some of the best songs ever written are about the jealously, the hopelessness, the lurching stomach and the downright unfairness of it all. My own personal favourite being "Is she really going out with him?" by Joe Jackson, where the singer questions his ex, what she is doing, and if she is with this other bloke there must be something going wrong.

That's just about how I will feel the first time I see Jose in his Manchester United blazer in his first press conference and then sitting on the bench against Leicester in the Community Shield and that dreadful day when he walks into Stamford Bridge (which will undoubtedly be the first game of the season). He'll be greeted by all the backroom staff who he'll hug, and then he will have his name sung by the faithful.

So does any of this matter? For me it does, and I suspect a fair few of you reading this.

There is no doubt that his third season was a disaster. From the preseason shambles, to his final departure. He was not blameless. Many of the problems were self-inflicted. A humble apology to the "Dr" may have got rid of a heap of problems, even if it was kept in house. The thing I do not understand is the club knew what they were getting when he returned so why didn't they back him when things went wrong. He wanted to buy players which we didn't get. He apparently wanted to get rid of certain players which he was not allowed to do. So principally he was managing under constraints.

I suspect that most managers do but you would have to ask why would you get one of the best managers around and then not let him manage? Or even worse let people who have no experience dictate what players he should have.

The question could also be reversed. Did Jose know the criteria when he came back? After all he had managed here before, and then at Madrid which presumably is similar to our style save for the hierarchy of football brains. That being said, their appointment at the beginning of last season does not point to a regime who knew what they were doing!

The recent extracts from Carlo Ancelotti's book hint at the level of alleged interference that our managers work under. Someone like Carlo managed at a club with an owner who wielded similar power so would not have been to fased by the regime at Chelsea. He has expressed regret that perhaps he should have put up more of a fight for Ray Wilkins when that particular rug was pulled from beneath him but if the dictum came from up high then he probably knew there was nothing he could do.

So why does Jose matter? Well we all know that he will

come back to haunt us. If he wins the league next season with Manchester United, none of us will be surprised. That being said the Premier League will be tougher next year, but we are aware that he knows how do get that particular job done. He has a huge amount of work to do there but there is no doubt he will get the financial backing he needs. Many have said that he won't play the youth. From memory Cech was 22 when he arrived, Courtois the same age when he displaced him, and Kurt even younger when introduced. Jose may be many things, but he is not stupid. Of course he will play Rashford, but how many of their other kids have excelled this season? He has a brilliant keeper, has a decent attack and needs reinforcements in defence and midfield... but he will know what's needed as no doubt he has been working on it since December.

The assumption is that Juan Mata will depart. Will he come back to us and indeed do we need him? I think we do need him, but cannot see Jose selling him back to us unless his opinion of him is so low that he will think it doesn't Mata.

We know what Jose is and what he gives you. I think at this time that we are a long way off winning the league again, but you can be certain these are two games Jose will go out to win. So if he does win the league next year it will mean he has stopped Pep, Arsene and Poch as well. His feud with the specialist in failure will be reignited and we all saw how well he got along with Pep. All major distractions and perhaps not conducive to a particularly quiet season at Old Trafford where the much maligned Europa League will be on offer.

So will I be against him next year? Only for two matches. I think he was hard done by and have said on several occasions that I would have got rid of the players not him. The completely pointless remainder of the season showed that actually there was no point in getting rid of him. Do people honestly think we would have gone down?

I think giving Jose the opportunity to rebuild would have been exciting. He could have removed those who allegedly didn't want to play for him and rebuilt a squad desperately in need of updating. It will be interesting to see who he brings in at Manchester United because defenders and ball winning midfielders with engines are what we needed and still need. With the exception of Hazard, is there anyone else (outside of Cesar, Kurt and Willian) who is not replaceable? If some want to argue that Jose wouldn't use our talented youth team... well he was fighting for his job... and anyway neither did Guus in games that were meaningless. I do not count minutes here and there... but we have wasted a fantastic opportunity.

I really don't get the conspiracy theories that he wanted to go to Man U all the time and so engineered his exit. The guy is a winner, and his reputation was seriously tarnished by what happened. I might be on shaky ground however if De Bruyne and Lukaku turn up in the summer I suspect the press will have a field day.

The guy they drove out they are driving back in.

Obviously delighted that next year arguably two of the greatest coaches in the world are in England and the sound bites the false feuds and everything else will be in full swing. Does that mean we may have a chance of being under the radar? There is no European football and the chance of getting on with it. Well probably unless we don't get off to a flyer and then our manager will be sought out for the usual treatment although that back page is going to be very crowded place.

THE END

So the season has finished. Question is did it ever start? No transfers to get excited about, the loss of our most successful manager and, with the exception of one notable game, a season which would be instantly forgettable was it not for the fact of how bizarre the whole thing has been.

Through the debris, I'd like to give some awards. Last year was a straightforward player of the year, save, goal etc; this year, slightly different... albeit I will start with the obvious ones.

Player of the Year: Nobody argued that it had to be Willian. It's fair to say he has always been a fan favourite due mostly to the manner of his arrival. This year he seemed to be the only player who seemed to ignore the dressing room implosion. Topping off his displays and rising to cult status when he pointed at his champions badge when being taunted by fans of the third best team in England.

Goal of the Season: Up until Eden Hazard had his own mini goal of the season tournament, for me it would have been Willian's goal against Newcastle. It was a sweeping move from a Newcastle corner, wonderful interplay involving Costa... and Willian arriving late to score. There is however no doubting that Eden's goal against Liverpool was a thing of absolute beauty. It was a perfect example of what he can do when he is fit his head is in the right place and nobody cynically hacks him down.

Save of the season: Cancelled.

Manager of the Season: Steve Holland. He was in charge for the first game following Jose's departure and oversaw a fine display from 11 guys who less than a week earlier didn't seem capable of kicking a football. A real miracle worker.

Atmosphere of the season: There is no doubting the crowd for the game at home against the third best team in England was something special. A job well done. The crowd in the aforementioned home game against Sunderland however were superb. Letting the players know what they thought of them and rightly so. The homemade Rat banners aside… chanting "where were you when we were shit?" after we scored was priceless. Joint second is our away support. Consistently brilliant.

Most improved player: Kurt Zouma. Up until his injury he was becoming the part. It is a fair criticism of Jose that he didn't promote the youth enough, but he put Kurt in and stuck with him. We all hope that he recovers and starts off from where he left off. He also seemed to get it. While others have floundered, he seemed to understand what playing for Chelsea was all about.

Wasted opportunity of the season: With nothing to play for, for the last quarter of the season the refusal/reluctance to play (subject to injuries) one of Baba, Kenedy, RLC, Traore for the remaining games for me has been inexcusable. To finish a rubbish season and not to have developed one player to first team status is negligent. How frustrating was it to see how natural Tomori was in the last game of the season (albeit in his wrong position) and wonder where he was 5/6 games ago.

Highlight of the season: The final whistle against Leicester bringing to an end a season which had been a let down on so many levels.

Low point of the season: Losing Jose. End of. Whatever the rights and wrongs of what happened with Jose, it is a great shame that it ended as it did. As I have said, it cannot be right for those players to simply stop playing. None of us know what support Jose got but those players should be playing for you me and the badge on the front of their shirt.

Steadying the ship award: Captain Guus, with the most over used cliché throughout his tenure.

Treading Water award: It was with a resigned shrug that I heard Guus talk in his last presser again about how he saved us from relegation. That's as maybe, but then what? Not a lot. Two wins in our last 12 games. One win at home under his guidance. With nothing to lose we played like a team with everything to lose. No adventure, slow ponderous and frankly dull. Ultimately we played like a 10th place team we ended up as.

Statistic of the Season: No goals conceded in the first 15 minutes of any premier league game.

Most disappointing game: The Everton defeat in the FA Cup. It would be hard to think of a more flat and directionless performance. I excuse Diego. He tried and got no protection from the referee and in the end just got fed up with it all and frankly who can blame him. The defeat at home to Bournemouth was also hard to take because if we are honest when we left that ground that day we knew there was no way back for the Special One.

Funniest moment of the season: Doing the double over the second best team in England despite having our worst season in over 20 years. In a season where we managed not a single victory over nine of our 19 opponents we still managed to win home and away against them. Classic.

Most pointless transfer of the season: I would say the most hotly contested award of them all. Whilst not a fully-fledged transfer you would have to say it is Pato. Not fit for months and then not fit for purpose. You would have to give an honourable mention to Papa. It is never going to happen but it would be lovely for the powers that be to actually explain the rationale behind the last two transfer windows.

Hands behind the back whilst defending award: Brana. A well-earned retention of this particular trophy.

Signing of the season: Potentially Conte but with the huge proviso that he is allowed to manage. I know it is the "modern" way for players to be given to the manager to work with but I have no doubt he would have set out some players he would like.

Tweet of the Season: "He'll be gone by Easter", my

tweet following the appointment of Claudio Ranieri.

Fans of the season: The away support and the various people who created and made happen all those wonderful flags and displays, from Osgood to Terry. We get bundles of cr@p as a club but some of the things the fans do go under the radar and they make supporting the club easier by their pride and efforts.

END OF SEASON PLAYER REPORT

Courtois

The guy has been unrecognisable from the keeper who arrived after 3 years at Atletico. At the beginning of last season, it was clear the decision to promote him over Petr Cech was sound so as to ensure he signed his new contract and remained at the club for the foreseeable. His season has been both interrupted and very average. There is no way a goalkeeper as good as him has become so poor. He has played behind a shambles of a team but his strange positioning and at times apparent lack of awareness have meant if he stays a lot more will be expected of him going forward. Stories of unrest behind the scenes may have also taken their toll.

Begovic

We are so lucky to have a keeper who arguably could walk into most sides in the Premier League as the back-up. He was apparently promised more game time but will ultimately have played more because of two sending offs and an injury to TC but less because we played our "strongest" team in the cups. Keepers will always suffer by not playing regularly and it's fair to say he may have done better in some games, but behind that defence Banks and Shilton would have struggled... playing together! Sadly however, his flap at Anfield will all he will be remembered for.

Brana

I feel bad criticising a guy who gives everything for the cause but he's had a really poor season. He was a shadow of himself at the beginning of the season and, despite being regularly taken to the cleaners, retained his position as Jose stayed loyal. It did him no favours, and whilst he played better at centre half his lack of guidance for some of the younger players is strange. A great servant but like many a very poor season.

Cesar

During the final days of Jose, Azpi was arguably the best defender in the back four. At last switched to right back he appeared to have struggled. I may be alone in this view but he may have been badly affected by Jose going. He was one of the trusted ones and will have missed the man (as most of us do). He much like Willian always gave everything and once we were safe finally "gave in". A decent season, and definitely our best and most consistent defender which is not a hard competition to win!

Gary Cahill

Very much second choice when Kurt was fit. He always comes across as a confidence player and I think struggles with constant changes in the back four. It is fair to say that his performance with Brana in Paris was one of the best rear guard actions of the season. Never gives anything less than 100% but like most of the back four this season has struggled and certainly not looked at his best.

JT

Last year was always going to be a hard act to follow and sadly it has proved impossible. A really poor start to the season but then regained form and looked to be back to somewhere near his best. The injuries coupled with his apparent exit from the club dominated matters since February, but no one will forget his crowd dive following his 97th minute goal against Everton. His presence on the pitch is always a bonus, but at times he like the rest of the team has looked lost. A club legend, with maybe one last hurrah in him

Zouma

A player who puts pay to the myth that Jose never plays kids. He was starting to look the part before his injury. His, at times, tactical naivety was a case of him learning on the job but his tough tackling and 100% commitment made him a real stand out this season not to mention that blistering pace. Let's hope he's back soon.

Matt Miazga

Apart from selling shirts, it is difficult to know what his addition to the squad was meant to achieve other than greatly piss off a whole list of equally talented young players. When he was signed there were eyebrows raised from across the pond. Despite his youth and international caps a promising debut was followed by a horror 45 minutes in Swansea. A subsequent benching behind Obi tells you everything you need to know.

Baba

This could be a whole chapter. He is young and raw and the subject of much divided opinion. Not trusted at all by Jose, he has produced some distinctly average performances but going forward his crossing is a vast improvement on both our other full backs. At times he has defended well and he looked the part in Paris. He has however shown Chelsea's utter folly of ditching first Ryan Bertrand and then Filipe Luis. Worth another season but the for price we paid he shouldn't be learning on the job...not the club's finest piece of business.

Cesc

So he is great before Christmas and disappears after it. Not this year. Wrongly suspected of being the "rat" his form has massively improved post Jose. Is that because we have played fewer games that mattered, or was he someone who was massively out of form and then regained it? Many will never forgive his past, but he has shown more mettle than some and it's not his fault his minders went AWOL this year. He is not fast and he is not the greatest tackler, but he seems to care and has finished the season well. He could flourish under Conte.

Matic

The poor guy has been a shadow of his former self. I still think he has never recovered from the sending off against Burnley but crikey that's over a year ago. One hears stories that he was one of Jose's victims and his treatment may have turned some against the Special one. Being hauled off after being a substitute will not have helped. It's hard to say he's much better post Jose, but one of the sadder sights of this season, and there have been many, has been watching his fall from grace. His last couple of games were a return to form, but this non celebration after his goal at Sunderland may mean he is on his way.

Mikel

He was nowhere to be seen in the first part of the season and then first name on the team sheet for Guus. The ultimate Marmite player for Chelsea fans. I like him and he has shown why he is one of the best squad players you can have. He is not however a central defender!

RLC

The clamour for game time and he finally gets it. I would say that he has not been what many expected. Naively it was thought he'd come in and set the Premier League alight. He needs time and his getting it. He's done well in a struggling team and he has proved that he is too good for youth football but not yet good enough for our first team. I say that with the caveat he is getting there and I would have preferred he like others had had more game time. All that being said, let's hope he is around next year and not loaned out and maybe actually played in his right position.

Kenedy

A great prospect who should have had more game time. I suspect that if Conte plays with wing backs this boy may be seen a lot next season. He is no defender, but his pace is a weapon. He looks the real deal if slightly raw. He is one for the future and I want to see more.

Ramires (Ray Mears)

A sad departure. We got good money for him and we needed to make space for RLC. The season was patchy, and it's hard to remember very much involvement for him. He will however always be a legend.

Willian

Not a huge amount of competition, but player of the year by a country mile. Without him and his goals earlier on this season we would have been in even more trouble and disarray. He never stopped trying, even when those around him quite plainly did not give a damn. His free kicks became a huge weapon, and his goal at home to Porto one of the few highlights this season. A top player.

Pedro

A guy who gives everything, and a decent player but not at all what I think we needed when we bought him. He is a live wire and is a really good finisher. He has suffered from injuries but with the exception of an absolute stinker against WBA at home has performed well.

Costa

Possibly one of the main players to give up on Jose. The level of his performances pre and post Jose point to that being the case. His lacklustre hiding compared to his running and chasing in the second part of the season being the hardest of evidence. As with last year, he has suffered from ridiculous trial by media when others get away with leg-breaking tackles. He snarls and pushes to the limit, but actually does no damage except to his team mates when he is suspended. At Everton he got no protection, got kicked from pillar to post and finally snapped. He'd had enough and he may well leave. A fully fit engaged Costa for a whole season would be a sight to behold but I just don't think we will ever see that.

Eden

That wasn't his best season was it? He was overweight, unfit and not very good at the beginning of the campaign. Missing decent chances can be forgiven, but his apparent attitude and a body language that stunk did not endear him to many. I recall at home to Liverpool he looked like he'd rather be anywhere than where he was. Then there were the injuries. The manner of his exit from the pitch against Leicester and his apparent spat with Jose were low points which turned many against him. He then came back and left the field against both Palace and PSG. Obviously not fit, but as our best player asked to participate and suffered ridiculous abuse. I sincerely believe he was not fit hence the situation but this was as big a fall from grace as Matic until his late season renaissance which culminated in two stunning goals. Fingers crossed he is with us next season

Remy

Strangely treated under Jose and then just woeful when given an opportunity. His last game (and it probably will be), when he played for 18 minutes and disappeared with a reoccurrence of lord knows what summed up an awful season. When on song he looks the business, but something happened and he has looked disinterested for most of this season. Not one of our stars.

Falcao

Legal reasons prevent me from speculating why he is at the club. A quite ludicrous signing. Scored a great goal. Anything I am missing?

Pato

Legal reasons prevent me from speculating why he is at the club. A quite ludicrous signing. Scored a penalty. Anything I am missing?

Traore

A real bright spark in an awful season. He has an eye for a goal, is quick and a real prospect. Hasn't played as much at the end of the season because... answers on a postcard. A wasted opportunity somehow stuck behind a lame duck (pardon the pun). There is something seriously wrong at our football club to allow that to happen. Let's hope he gets more game time next season.

Jose

As referenced in The Long Goodbye chapter.

Guus

"Steadied the ship". "Didn't have as strong a squad as last time". "The players love him". All of the above. He stopped us going down (was that never going to happen?) He got us playing some decent football but his paternal demeanour accounted for that abject surrender at

Goodison. At the end he seemed to be doing what he'd been asked to do by Conte/the powers that be. His team selections and lack of playing time for some of the youth a mystery unless he was under orders. My only question is where we are now? Is that any different to where we would have been had Jose stayed?

*****

Printed in Great Britain
by Amazon